RAND PRINCIPAL PREPARATION SERIES



# Using State-Level Policy Levers to Promote Principal Quality

## Lessons from Seven States Partnering with Principal Preparation Programs and Districts

Susan M. Gates, Ashley Woo, Lea Xenakis, Elaine Lin Wang, Rebecca Herman, Megan Andrew, Ivy Todd

RAND CORPORATION

Commissioned by Wallace

For more information on this publication, visit www.rand.org/t/RRA413-1

**Library of Congress Cataloging-in-Publication Data** is available for this publication.
ISBN: 978-1-9774-0516-6

Published by the RAND Corporation, Santa Monica, Calif.


*Cover images: Suwannar Kawila/EyeEm/GettyImages and jweise/GettyImages*

# Preface

States play a role in fostering an environment that develops and supports effective school principals. Prior research has highlighted opportunities to enhance state efforts to improve principal quality through a range of policy levers, especially by promoting improvements to principal preparation (Davis, 2016; Manna, 2015). The Wallace Foundation launched the University Principal Preparation Initiative (UPPI) in July 2016. The four-year, $48.5-million initiative supports seven universities, their district and state partners, and mentor programs to redesign the universities' principal preparation programs according to evidence-based practices. State partners to the seven universities committed to review policies that affect university-based principal preparation and to also work with stakeholders to consider policy changes.

RAND Corporation researchers are analyzing the implementation of UPPI and changes to the design and delivery of preparation programs. RAND's first report on UPPI (Wang et al., 2018) documented findings from the first year of UPPI implementation. The final report for the project, on UPPI implementation and program change, is scheduled for publication in 2022.

This special topic report draws generalizable lessons from UPPI states about the role of state policy efforts focused on the principalship. Findings will be of interest to state officials striving to improve principal quality statewide. We distilled cross-site themes from an in-depth look at how each state partner uses state policy levers described by Manna (2015). The report describes themes about the use of the state policy levers and policy change, illustrating possible approaches to state policy action focused on the principalship, as well as facilitators and barriers to state-level change. State-specific profiles about the use of policy levers for each of the seven UPPI states are provided in an appendix to the main report (available at www.rand.org/t/RRA413-1).

This research was conducted prior to the COVID-19 pandemic. As of September 2020, the pandemic has not changed the state role in improving principal quality, though it may have elevated the complexity of the job principals do and heightened the need for states to actively promote principal quality. The longer-term implications of COVID-19 on state functions remain to be seen, but we anticipate the lessons we present in this report are enduring.

This research was undertaken by RAND Education and Labor, a division within the RAND Corporation that conducts research on early childhood through postsecondary education programs, workforce development, and programs and policies affecting workers, entrepreneurship, and financial literacy and decisionmaking. The study was funded by The Wallace Foundation, which seeks to foster improvements in learning and enrichment for young people and the vitality of the arts for everyone.

More information about RAND can be found at www.rand.org. Questions about this report should be directed to sgates@rand.org, and questions about RAND Education and Labor should be directed to educationandlabor@rand.org.

# Contents

# Figures, Tables, and Boxes

## Figures



## Tables

## Boxes

# Summary

Effective school leaders, particularly principals, are associated with better outcomes for students and schools (Branch, Hanushek, and Rivkin, 2012; Grissom, Kalogrides, and Loeb, 2015; Leithwood et al., 2004). Principals help set school vision and culture, which support teacher effectiveness and ultimately can help improve student achievement. Given the demonstrated importance of effective school leadership, stakeholders interested in improving the quality of public education have worked to build knowledge about strategies that principal preparation programs, districts, and states can use to improve principal quality.

State policymakers, including state leaders, districts, and professional associations, play a role in fostering an environment that supports the development of effective school principals, with the broad policy objective of achieving high principal quality across the state. Research has shown that states often seek to influence principal quality either by establishing policy agendas that address school principals or by using available policy levers (Manna, 2015). At the same time, the state role must be understood in the broader historical context of education policy in the United States, which emphasizes local control over education and is strongly influenced by nongovernmental organizations (Smarick and Squire, 2014; Weiss and McGuinn, 2016).

## Focus of This Study

In this report, we examine how seven states use state policy levers to advance policy change to improve the quality of school principals. These states are all actively engaging in a collaborative initiative focused on principal preparation program redesign. We consider the following questions, drawing on data about the use of various policy levers in the states:

- How does a state's context shape its use of policy levers to improve principal quality?
- What policy levers are states using, how are the levers used, and what policy changes have states made that affect the way levers are used?
- What supports the effective use of policy levers?

- What are the barriers to and facilitators of policy change?

All seven states in the study were part of The Wallace Foundation's University Principal Preparation Initiative (UPPI). Launched in 2016, UPPI is supporting seven university-based principal preparation programs to work in collaboration with their district and state partners to redesign and improve the programs to better support the development of effective principals. The programs were chosen for the initiative, in part, because they were located in states that had favorable conditions for supporting principal quality. In addition, the programs had expressed interest in and already conducted some initial work toward redesigning their principal preparation programs. The UPPI programs and their respective states are Albany State University (Georgia), Florida Atlantic University (Florida), North Carolina State University (North Carolina), San Diego State University (California), the University of Connecticut (Connecticut), Virginia State University (Virginia), and Western Kentucky University (Kentucky).

We drew on three data sources for this analysis: (1) biannual interviews with UPPI participants, (2) interviews with state-level stakeholders across the seven UPPI states, and (3) relevant secondary data, such as state plans, state licensure requirements, state legislation, reports from state departments of education, and research literature on school leadership.

In this report, we focus on seven policy levers that states can use to improve school leadership. The first six of these were drawn from research as described by Manna (2015), and the seventh was derived from Grissom, Mitani, and Woo (2019):

- setting principal standards
- recruiting aspiring principals into the profession
- licensing new and veteran principals
- approving and overseeing principal preparation programs
- supporting principals' growth with professional development
- evaluating principals
- using leader tracking systems to support analysis of aspiring and established school leaders' experiences and outcomes.

## Findings

Table S.1 summarizes key policy actions associated with each lever and the prevalence of use of key policy lever activities in UPPI states. We found that standards, licensure, program approval and oversight, and professional development are core levers for which key activities are performed by all or most states.

**Table S.1**
**Prevalence of Key Policy Actions, by Policy Lever**

| Policy Lever | Key Policy Actions | Prevalence of Use Among UPPI States |
|---|---|---|
| Standards | • Adopt state standards for school principals<br>• Promote the use of state standards | • All<br>• All |
| Recruitment of aspiring leaders | • Establish prerequisites for program participation<br>• Subsidize participation in pre-service programs<br>• Encourage effective program recruitment practice | • All<br>• Few<br>• Most |
| Licensure | • Determine licensure pathways<br>• Determine licensure requirements | • All<br>• All |
| Program approval and oversight | • Determine types of providers that can offer programs<br>• Establish criteria for program approval/renewal<br>• Approve programs<br>• Specify program content/structure | • All<br>• All<br>• All<br>• Most |
| Professional development | • Establish requirements for principal professional development<br>• Support or offer principal professional development | • Most<br>• All |
| Evaluation | • Establish content criteria<br>• Establish process expectations<br>• Establish reporting requirements | • Few<br>• Few<br>• Few |
| Leader tracking systems | • Support data systems for tracking aspiring and current principals | • None |

NOTE: Few = 1–3 of the states; most = 4–6 of the states.

## Features of the state context influence opportunities to improve principal quality

Our review of state policy efforts confirms findings from prior research that multiple actors play a role in developing and implementing state policy to improve principal quality (Kingdon, 1984; Manna, 2015). We found that three roles are especially important: setting direction through legislation and funding, shaping the direction more precisely through regulation and oversight, and providing resources and services. Although there are clear formal leaders for each role (e.g., the legislature is responsible for developing legislation), a number of other stakeholders are informally involved in each role. For example, the governor, department of education, professional standards board, and nonstate entities influence the direction of legislation.

### *State Policy Actors*

**State legislatures** shape statewide principal policy through legislation and appropriation of funds. Some legislatures are more hands-off, delegating details of policy implementation to **state departments of education** or **professional educator standards boards**. Other legislatures craft highly specific laws, leaving little flexibility for the department of education to further shape policy direction. The responsibility for licensing administrators and approving preparation programs falls to either the

**state department of education** or (where they exist) **professional educator standards boards**. In addition, **regional cooperatives** and **county offices** exist in some, but not all, of the states in our study. Where they exist, they play a key role in providing services such as principal professional development, especially in small or rural districts. In some states, these entities may offer state-approved preparation or professional development programs. In all seven states in our study, a wide range of **nongovernmental organizations**—including **professional associations, higher education councils** or **university systems**, and **nonprofits**—influence school leadership policy by informing legislation, advising on implementation, and serving on tasks forces and panels. **Governors** also influence principal quality through the development of specific initiatives and oversight of state departments of education and their authority to appoint state education board members and the superintendent of education.

#### *The Pathway to the Principalship*

Drawing on interview data and descriptive, publicly available documents, we mapped the basic pathway through which aspiring leaders become principals in UPPI states (see Figure S.1) via a principal preparation program. The figure highlights two features of the pathway that have potential implications for the use of policy levers: (1) multiple stages of licensure that allow for a sequence of requirements and (2) alternative pathways to the principalship that do not involve a state-approved preparation program.

#### *Agenda Status*

Consistent with Manna's findings (2015, p. 12), stakeholders we interviewed did not often mention school leadership as a top education priority for their state. This **low agenda status** can make it difficult to get legislators and other policymakers to act on an issue. At the same time, a lower profile comes with less scrutiny and controversy, and thus can help an issue get through the policy process and help anchor changes so that they are less vulnerable to being overturned.

### States use the policy levers in different ways

We examined the use of each of the seven policy levers in UPPI states and found that the levers are used by states in different ways.

We found that all UPPI states actively use **standards**, **licensure**, and **program approval and oversight** levers. All UPPI states have updated their **standards** since 2011 and make the standards visible to the public, districts, and other stakeholders. Our review of approaches to **licensure** identified three main state-level licensure policy choices: whether there is a license specific to the principalship, whether the state requires an assessment for licensure, and what other requirements candidates must meet for licensure. In all UPPI states, there is a state entity responsible for **program approval and oversight**. In three states, this responsibility is housed within an independent or semi-independent professional standards board; in the others, this responsibility falls

**Figure S.1**
**Pathway to the Principalship, Including a Multi-Staged Program Pathway and an Alternative Pathway**

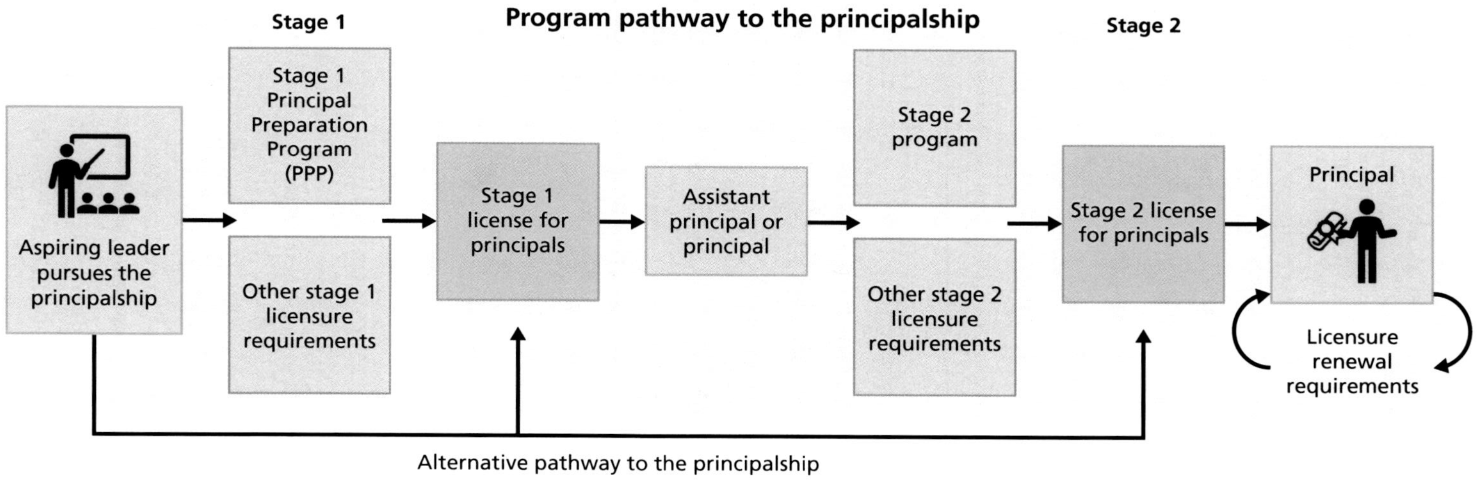

to the state board of education. All UPPI states have program approval standards, and almost all require programs to develop partnerships with school districts.

States also use the **recruitment**, **evaluation**, and **professional development** levers, but with more restraint. We did not find evidence that the **leader tracking system** lever is currently being used, although there is interest in it among the states we studied.

#### *The use of levers is influenced by the principal pathway structure*

We mapped the use of levers onto the pathway to the principalship (Figure S.2). The recruitment, evaluation, and professional development levers operate at the beginning or end of the pathway, whereas program approval and oversight and licensure operate at various points within the pathway. Standards operate across the entire pathway, and leader tracking systems have the potential to do so as well. The **structure of the pathway provides opportunities for policy action** related to school leadership. We observed that states with multi-staged leadership pathways develop different sets of expectations for programs and principal candidates in each stage of the process.

#### *States use mandates judiciously to influence principal quality*

Although some studies have recommended that states be more active and directive when using their policy levers (Davis, 2016), there are trade-offs between promoting principal quality through directive mandates and allowing program or district flexibility. Our review indicated that states tend to use mandates in areas where the direct target of a policy is an aspiring leader or a program and where the mandate is attached to a privilege or benefit the state is conferring on the target. All seven states use mandates in exercising program approval and oversight and principal licensure authority.

### State policy stakeholders provided insights into effective use of levers

To understand what supports the effective use of state policy levers, we asked stakeholders whether they agreed that their state was using levers effectively and what they perceived to be barriers and facilitators of effective use. We also considered how the interconnectedness of the levers can enhance their use and what other factors contribute to effective use.

**Factors That Appear to Facilitate the Effectiveness of Policy Levers**

- Interconnectedness
- Two-stage pathways
- Linking the lever to rigorous, evidence-based requirements
- Providing programs and districts with support to meet requirements
- Oversight
- Accountability
- Resources

#### *Stakeholders reported that some levers are used effectively*

Responses from state stakeholders suggest that states emphasize different combinations of levers. In no state did a majority of the stakeholders we interviewed report that the state was using all levers effec-

**Figure S.2**
**Policy Levers Mapped onto the Generalized Program Pathway to the Principalship**

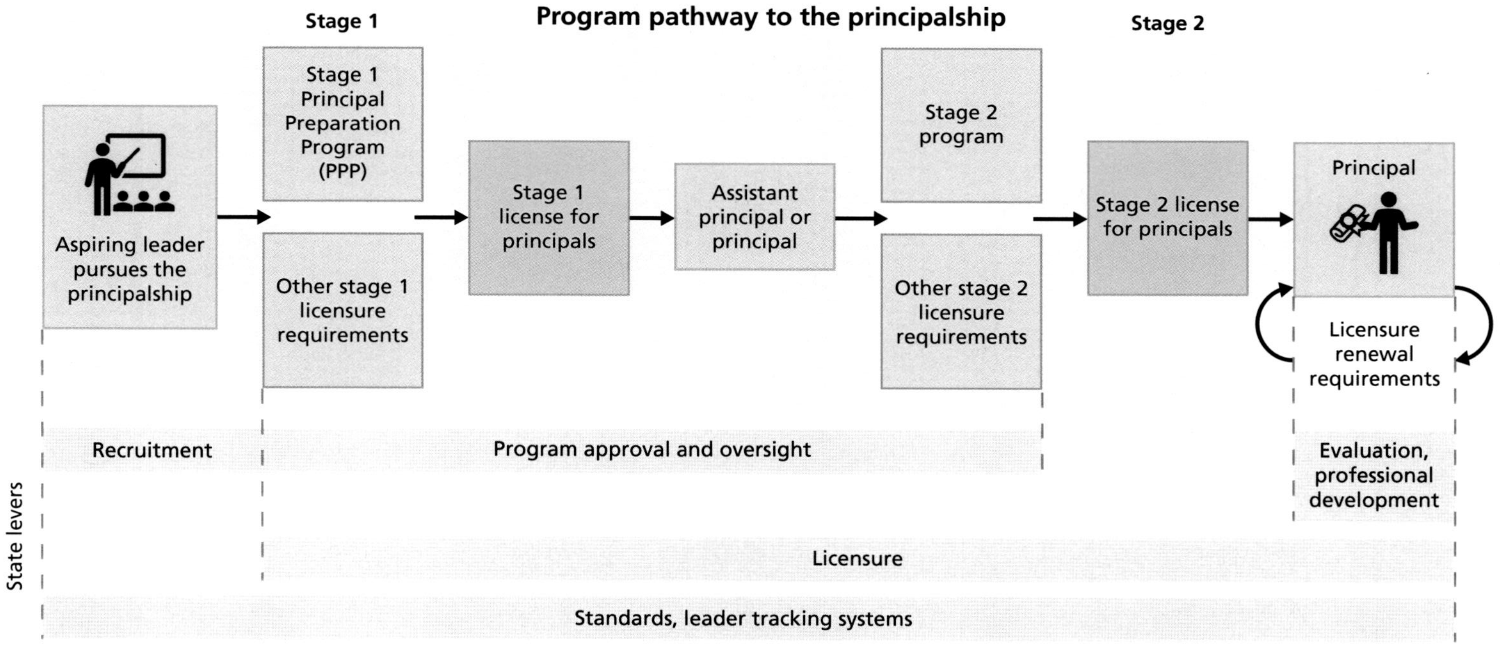

**Table S.2**
**Majority (50% or More) of Stakeholders Agreed That Use of Lever in State Is Effective, by Lever and by State**

| Policy Lever | California | Connecticut | Florida | Georgia | Kentucky | North Carolina | Virginia |
|---|---|---|---|---|---|---|---|
| Standards | X | X | X | X | X | X | X |
| Recruitment of aspiring leaders | | | | | | X | |
| Licensure | X | | X | X | | | X |
| Program approval and oversight | X | X | | X | X | | X |
| Professional development | | X | X | | | | X |
| Evaluation | | | X | | | | X |
| Leader tracking systems | | | | | | | |

NOTE: Responses were analyzed as Agree, Disagree, Neutral, or No response; lack of a mark indicating majority agreement should therefore not be interpreted as disagreement.

tively. As shown in Table S.2, the highest number of levers for which there was agreement on effective use was five. Perceptions of the effectiveness of the levers sometimes differed by stakeholder role, with stakeholder groups more likely to feel that a lever was being used effectively in cases where they had primary responsibility for the lever (i.e., it was within their sphere of control).

Across states, there was agreement that the standards lever was being effectively used to promote principal quality. Stakeholders in five states also felt that the program approval lever was being used effectively.

Across states, most interviewee groups indicated that the leader tracking, evaluation, and recruitment levers are not used effectively. These perspectives about effective use could indicate either that the state is not using the lever at all or that the state is using the lever but not doing so effectively. The former appears to be the case with regard to leader tracking and evaluation, while the latter appears to be the case for the recruitment lever.

***Interconnections among levers can extend a lever's influence***

The levers are interconnected. This means that the opportunity to use one lever may be influenced by the degree of policy action that has been taken with another lever. For example, standards have their greatest influence when used as an alignment framework for licensure, program approval, professional development, and evaluation. The influence of one lever on another can move in both directions. For example, licensure requirements make program approval requirements more influential, and program approval requirements create opportunities for licensure requirements.

Among the states in our study, the interconnectedness among levers manifested in three main ways: (1) the use of one lever references or ties to the use of others (e.g., a state embeds standards in program approval and licensure requirements); (2) one lever draws authority from use of another lever (e.g., the influence of a weaker lever such as standards is bolstered by its connection to a stronger lever such as licensure); and (3) changes in the use of one lever trigger or require changes in the use of a different lever (e.g., changes to standards trigger changes to the program approval process and licensure regulations).

#### *Other factors appear to influence the effectiveness of lever use*

Interviewees identified several other factors associated with effective lever use:

- **Evidence-based, rigorous requirements positively affect stakeholders' perceptions of a lever's effectiveness.** Interviewees emphasized that levers must be connected to high standards or evidence-based requirements in order to be effective; in comparison, requirements that were seen as simply "jumping through hoops," setting a low bar, or adding layers of bureaucracy were not seen as effective.
- **Programs and districts may need state support** to meet rigorous state requirements. In particular, we observed that stakeholders perceived lever use as more effective when state policymakers are sensitive to capacity constraints and thus design more-comprehensive policies that include both rigorous requirements and supports to carry out these requirements. For example, stakeholders in Georgia noted that the state has used a consistent evaluation tool for years that is also mandated by law. Training on the evaluation tool, paid for by Race to the Top, has allowed for a deeper focus on evaluation in the state.
- **Oversight, accountability, and resources all support policy implementation and effectiveness.** For example, when California rolled out a new assessment for preparation program candidates, passing the assessment became a requirement for licensure and program completion. The state provided many opportunities for preparation program providers to obtain support to modify their programs to prepare candidates for the assessment. Stakeholders in several states mentioned the importance of expertise in oversight, particularly in program approval.

### States face challenges in implementing policy change but can also draw on facilitators to support change

We also learned about challenges to and facilitators of state-level policy change to promote principal quality.

States face challenges in implementing policy changes to better support principal quality, including limited **staff time and resources**, as well as **competing priorities** that can relegate leadership issues to the backburner. **Turnover of state leaders** can delay or challenge policy changes. An emphasis on **local autonomy**—giving districts and programs flexibility to identify their leadership needs and priorities—and **stakeholder buy-in** also influences the policies that states put forth and the mechanisms—a combination of mandates, incentives, supports—they use. In a context that values local control, states may be reluctant to "overreach."

Certain factors appear to facilitate policy change, however. Chief among them is **early and meaningful engagement of stakeholders**, which helps ensure buy-in of newly crafted policies, and which helps expand state capacity to implement these policies. **Leveraging stakeholders' expertise**—for example, through task forces and advisory boards—can help supplement and expand state capacity. Interviewees also suggested that **low agenda status** can actually facilitate change because the absence of strong opposition can help move and sustain policy efforts. **Leveraging related statewide efforts** can help move school leadership efforts forward. For example, in California, the development of a performance-based assessment for school administration licensure candidates built upon a similar performance-based assessment for teacher candidates. **National policies and guidelines**, such as national standards for school leaders, can also be influential external drivers of change. In addition, **mandates, combined with supports or information**, appear to be preferred mechanisms for change. **Offering resources or professional development** with voluntary take-up of new policy or practice can also be a channel for change. For example, in Connecticut, the department of education encouraged and supported, but did not require, principal preparation programs' use of the Quality Measures review process.

## Recommendations

Considering the findings summarized above, we emphasize the following recommendations for states interested in improving school leadership statewide:

### When setting policy priorities to improve principal quality, consider the mix of policy options available

Because the state policy levers are interconnected, and their use is influenced by the state's pathway to the principalship as well as other aspects of the state context, there is no one-size-fits-all approach to revising state policy to improve principal quality. States should consider whether there are ways to leverage or enhance existing mandates by linking them more strongly to principal standards and to one another and associating them with rigorous expectations. States should also reflect on whether existing mandates are effective. Consistent and aligned use of different policy levers can promote a coherent state strategy for improving principal quality.

**Considerations for States Interested in Improving School Leadership Statewide**

- Consider the mix of policy options available and how existing mandates can be leveraged or enhanced.
- Build state-level engagement and expertise on principal quality.
- Couple mandates with information, resources, and support.
- Be opportunistic: Link principal initiatives to state education priorities and existing initiatives.

### Identify opportunities to build stakeholder engagement and state-level expertise on principal quality

Limited resources—in terms of funding, expertise, and time—can constrain the capacity of state education agencies. But these agencies do not define the entirety of state capacity. Other state stakeholders, including professional standards boards, principal associations, and regional education cooperatives, among many others, can be leveraged in a variety of ways to effectively expand the state's capacity and can sometimes serve as drivers of policy change. States can support or amplify such efforts by providing a forum or mechanism for information-sharing (such as professional learning community meetings, think tanks, or convenings). State agencies can also help build other organizations' and individuals' knowledge, expertise, and agency by identifying and inviting new stakeholders to serve on committees or participate in convenings and by disseminating information about best practices and resources.

### When using state mandates to drive principal quality, couple them with information, resources, and supports

If used judiciously, mandates regarding licensure, evaluation, and program approval requirements can be a powerful way to drive improvement to principal quality. But when a policy is targeting changes in behavior of aspiring principals, principals, districts, or programs, it will be effective only if those actors can meet the expectations of the policy. Coupling mandates with resources and information to help develop that capacity—by funding programs with state resources, by promoting peer networks, and by developing information resources that stakeholders can tap—can increase the odds of success for a state mandate.

### Be opportunistic: Link principal initiatives to key state education priorities and build on related initiatives

Among the most significant examples of policy change we observed in UPPI states were efforts that build on or leverage prior statewide efforts focused on teachers, students, or broad kindergarten through grade 12 (K–12) priorities. We also observed examples in which external drivers, such as new national policies or guidelines, facilitated change by promoting consideration of policy actions. This suggests that state actors should be opportunistic in building off existing policy efforts focused on teachers and consider whether and when something similar might be developed and implemented with a focus on principals. A related strategy is to tie or frame a potential policy change with reference to another high-level state or national initiative.

## Acknowledgments

This research relied on information gathered as part of a multi-year evaluation of The Wallace Foundation's University Principal Preparation Initiative (UPPI). We are grateful to the university-based leads at each of the seven participating universities, as well as their partner organizations—districts, state agencies, and mentor programs. We are also grateful to the numerous other state officials and state-level actors across the UPPI states who spoke with us about educational priorities and efforts to improve principal quality initiatives in their states. We appreciate the efforts of the UPPI project managers who helped us identify appropriate state-level interviewees and schedule interviews and other data collection activities. This report would not have been possible without the input of all these individuals.

We are grateful to Paul Manna for providing feedback on a detailed outline of this report and to Elaine Allensworth, Barnett Barry, Dominic Brewer, Ann Clark, Lindsay Daugherty, Ellen Goldring, Erika Hunt, and Paul Manna for their feedback on earlier drafts of this report.

We would like to thank our contacts at The Wallace Foundation, who provided important input on the overall study and this report. We benefited from feedback from Elizabeth Ty Wilde, Pamela Mendels, Jody Spiro, Bronwyn Bevan, Edward Pauly, Andrew Cole, Aiesha Eleusizov, Rochelle Herring, Nicholas Pelzer, Lucas Bernays Held, and Will Miller.

We are indebted to Kristin Leuschner for assisting with the overall framing of the report, developing key graphics, and helping with the structure of the report, to James Torr for a careful copyedit and to Ninna Gudgell for formatting, editing, and design help.

## Abbreviations

| | |
|---|---|
| CAEP | Council for the Accreditation of Educator Preparation |
| CalAPA | California Administrator Performance Assessment |
| CTC | California Commission on Teacher Credentialing |
| EPSB | Educator Professional Standards Board (Kentucky) |
| ESSA | Every Student Succeeds Act |
| K–12 | kindergarten through grade 12 |
| KDE | Kentucky Department of Education |
| NC DPI | North Carolina Department of Public Instruction |
| NC PFP | North Carolina Principal Fellows Program |
| NELP | National Educational Leadership Preparation |
| PSEL | Professional Standards for Educational Leaders |
| SBDM | school-based decisionmaking |
| SELECT | School Educational Leadership Enhancement Committee Task Force (Florida) |
| TP3 | Transforming Principal Preparation Program (North Carolina) |
| UCEA | University Council for Educational Administration |
| UPPI | University Principal Preparation Initiative |

CHAPTER ONE

# Introduction

Effective school leadership is associated with better outcomes for students and schools, including but not limited to improvements in student achievement (Branch, Hanushek, and Rivkin, 2012; Grissom, Kalogrides, and Loeb, 2015; Leithwood et al., 2004). Principals help set school vision and culture, which support teacher effectiveness and ultimately can help improve student achievement. Over the course of their career, a single principal can influence hundreds of teachers and students. But not all schools and districts are getting the principal quality they seek. Although there is no evidence of principal vacancies per se, a national survey revealed that less than half of public school districts nationwide were at least moderately satisfied with the pool of principal candidates (Gates et al., 2020). In another survey effort, 80 percent of superintendents reported a need to improve principal preparation programs (Davis, 2016). Manna (2015) has argued that improvements in the quality of school principals can have a "multiplier effect" across schools and districts and be particularly cost-effective. States are beginning to recognize this. For example, motivated in part by this base of evidence on the importance of school principals, over the past decade the state of Illinois has undertaken comprehensive state action to improve principal quality through a focus on principal preparation (Haller, Hunt, and Baron, 2019a).

Those interested in improving the quality of public education have worked to build knowledge about strategies that preparation programs, districts, and states can use to improve principal quality. Principal preparation programs can look to research-based recommendations for improving programs by emphasizing leadership skills that have been shown to be related to student and school success, providing comprehensive clinical experiences linked to coursework, and engaging in selective admission practices (Davis, 2016; Fry, Bottoms, and O'Neill, 2005; Hess and Kelly, 2007; Sherman and Cunningham, 2006). Districts[1] can draw on evidence about the effectiveness of comprehensive principal pipelines that promote principal quality through strategic consideration of leader standards, high-quality pre-service preparation, strategic hiring, and

[1] Throughout the report, we use the term *district* to refer to local education agencies, local units of administration, or consortia of school districts.

evaluation and support (Gates et al., 2019), as well as targeted evidence about specific initiatives that address pieces of that pipeline (Herman et al., 2017).

State policymakers and other state policy influencers play a role in fostering an environment that supports school leaders and helps districts and preparation programs develop and support effective principals. The broad policy objective of state involvement is to achieve high principal quality across the state. The relevant stakeholders interested in this goal include state leaders, districts, professional associations, principal preparation programs, and aspiring leaders, among others (Haller, Hunt, and Baron, 2019b). Each of these stakeholders has some influence on the pathway (see Figure 1.1) one takes from a teacher to a principal and/or the principal's effectiveness once on the job.

Augustine et al. (2009) describe the most promising state efforts to improve school leadership as those that are comprehensive—addressing a range of activities including standards, licensure, preparation, evaluation, and working conditions—and aligned across activities and state and district initiatives.[2]

Research, as summarized by Manna (2015), suggests that states can improve principal quality through

- "POLICY AGENDAS that address school principals along with other priorities"

**Figure 1.1**
**Generalized Pathway to the Principalship**

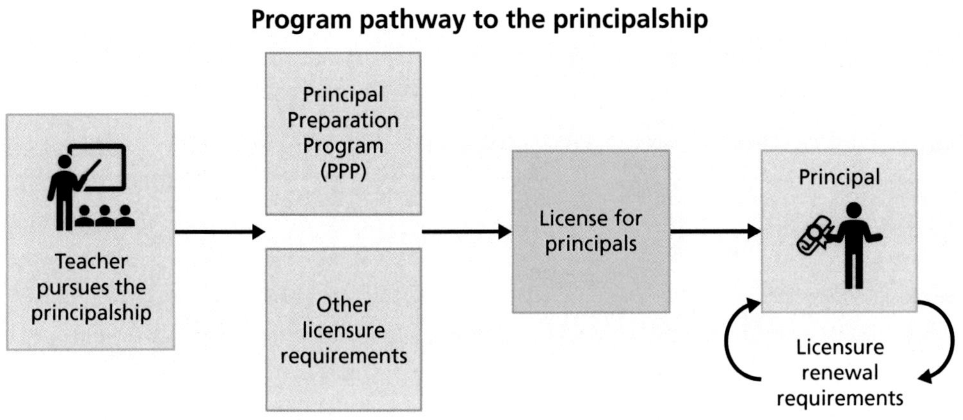


[2] Principal quality (or effectiveness) is a component of a broader policy objective of educator effectiveness, the focus of which is most commonly teachers. As a result, frameworks for state policy to promote teacher quality have similar elements, addressing preparation, alternative routes to certification, hiring, evaluation, compensation, and retention (California Department of Education, 2012; National Center for Teacher Quality, 2019).

- "POLICY LEVERS available to state leaders as they attempt to identify and train aspiring principals and support those already on the job" (p. 16, emphasis in the original).

States are relevant actors because they possess important funding, as well as constitutional and legislative authorities, that can be leveraged to influence principal quality. Notably, states have the authority to license or authorize individuals to be employed as public-school principals in the state and to approve the programs that prepare aspiring principals. But the state role is not limited to these formal authorities. State actors also have the ability to mobilize other levels of government, as well as nongovernmental organizations, in pursuit of state goals. Collectively, these inputs constitute state capacity on education policy matters generally and principal quality in particular (Moffitt et al., 2018).

That being said, there are also inherent limitations to the state role in education policy, which have implications for the state role in improving principal quality. Prior research has characterized the complexity of the U.S. education policy environment generally and resulting barriers to state-level influence (Moffitt et al., 2018). In the United States, education policy is made at the federal, state, and local levels. The state policy role in education has been limited by an emphasis on local control over kindergarten through grade 12 (K–12) education and involvement of nongovernmental organizations (Smarick and Squire, 2014; Weiss and McGuinn, 2016). Some argue that state actors in the education policy sphere have limited capacity to monitor and support what is being executed at the regional and local levels (Smarick and Squire, 2014). In the past few decades, with growing emphasis on content standards and equity, the work of state education agencies of overseeing and administering state systems has become "more than simply a technocratic exercise. SEA [state education agency] work is deeply political and contested" (Howley and Sturges, 2018, p. 14).

## Focus of This Report

In this report, we examine how seven states that are actively engaging in a collaborative initiative focused on principal preparation program redesign use state policy levers to advance policy change to improve the quality of school principals. We identify key themes about how state policy levers are used and draw generalizable insights for other states.

We consider the following questions, drawing on data about the use of various policy levers in the seven states:

- How does a state's context shape its use of policy levers to improve principal quality?

- What policy levers are states using, how are the levers used, and what policy changes have states made that affect the way levers are used?
- What supports the effective use of policy levers?
- What are the facilitators of and barriers to policy change?

We consider use of policy levers in the context of the pathway to the principalship illustrated in Figure 1.1. At different stages of the pathway, states have different opportunities to influence principal quality by targeting the behavior of different stakeholders, most notably

- aspiring principals
- principal preparation programs
- districts that hire and employ principals
- professional development providers
- principals.

When considering the use of policy levers, we focus on both the policy target of the lever and features of its use.

State profiles, in Appendix B to this report, describe how the policy levers are used in each of the seven states and illustrate the relationship between policy and context and the interconnections among levers. (Appendix B is available at www.rand.org/t/RRA413-1.)

In the remainder of this introduction, we provide contextual information about the states included in our study and then discuss seven state policy levers for influencing principal quality. We also provide a brief overview of our methods.

## The States Included in Our Study[3]

This study focuses on seven states (California, Connecticut, Florida, Georgia, Kentucky, North Carolina, and Virginia) that illustrate some unique as well as some generalizable conditions. We chose these states precisely because they offer optimal conditions in which to observe policy change to promote principal quality.

First, all seven states were focused on principal preparation prior to and during the study. Each of the states was identified by Davis (2016) as having a policy context supportive of high-quality principal preparation.[4] This is not the case across the United

---

[3] This section draws heavily from the introduction of Wang et al., 2018. Readers interested in more detail about the background of the University Principal Preparation Initiative and characteristics of the grantees are directed to that report for additional information.

[4] Davis (2016) identified three states (Illinois, Kentucky, and Tennessee) as having the most favorable policy conditions and ten other states (California, Connecticut, Florida, Georgia, Iowa, Massachusetts, North Carolina,

States: Davis (2016) found that many states do not use their authority to influence principal preparation as effectively as they could (p. 14).

Second, at the time of the study, a university principal preparation program in each of these seven states was part of The Wallace Foundation's University Principal Preparation Initiative (UPPI), a collaborative effort launched in 2016 to redesign and improve such programs to better support the development of effective principals. The programs were chosen, in part, because they had expressed interest in and already conducted some initial work toward redesigning their principal preparation programs. Participating programs, which were selected through a competitive process, have been collaborating with district and state partners to revise their programs to better incorporate features associated with program effectiveness. The UPPI programs and their respective states are

- Albany State University in Albany, Georgia
- Florida Atlantic University in Boca Raton, Florida
- North Carolina State University in Raleigh, North Carolina
- San Diego State University in San Diego, California
- University of Connecticut in Storrs, Connecticut
- Virginia State University in Petersburg, Virginia
- Western Kentucky University in Bowling Green, Kentucky.

While the university-based principal preparation programs lead the UPPI effort, each UPPI grantee also has a state partner, which is the organization that accredits that state's principal preparation programs. The state partners were, respectively,

- Georgia Professional Standards Commission
- Florida Department of Education
- North Carolina Department of Public Instruction
- California Commission on Teacher Credentialing
- Connecticut State Department of Education
- Virginia Department of Education
- Kentucky Education Professional Standards Board (which subsequently merged with the Kentucky Department of Education).

Given the involvement of the state partners, the seven states in this study may have been more deeply engaged in state-level change than many other states were. As part of their work with UPPI, UPPI state partners committed to work closely with the grantee programs—and their district partners—to facilitate UPPI and to organize state convenings to disseminate lessons learned from UPPI. They also agreed to partic-

---

Pennsylvania, Rhode Island, and Virginia) as having "conditions conducive to improving principal preparation" (p. 16).

ipate in Wallace-sponsored professional learning communities with leaders from other states—as well as UPPI university and district leaders—to share and develop strategies to improve principal preparation, and to review state policies that affect university-based principal preparation.

Although UPPI programs adhere to a broad set of common goals, the educational environment for these programs differs across states. UPPI states vary widely in terms of number and size of districts, as well as the degree of across-district variation in student and community characteristics (see Table 1.1).

**Table 1.1**
**Characteristics of the Local Context, by State**

| | California | Connecticut | Florida | Georgia | Kentucky | North Carolina | Virginia |
|---|---|---|---|---|---|---|---|
| Number of districts | 993 | 169 | 67 | 180 | 173 | 115 | 130 |
| Total student enrollment | 6,210,188 | 500,039 | 2,801,945 | 1,732,691 | 683,864 | 1,457,357 | 1,272,557 |
| Students per district | 6,254 | 2,959 | 41,820 | 9,626 | 3,953 | 12,673 | 9,789 |
| Number of districts serving 100,000 or more students | 2 | 0 | 8 | 3 | 0 | 2 | 1 |
| % of districts that are small (<10,000) | 83% | 95% | 43% | 79% | 94% | 69% | 80% |
| % of districts that are very small (<5,000) | 71% | 85% | 25% | 63% | 86% | 43% | 63% |
| % of districts that are rural | 34% | 38% | 30% | 58% | 52% | 63% | 51% |
| Average per-pupil spending | 11,893 | 20,426 | 9,555 | 10,242 | 10,238 | 9,077 | 11,908 |

SOURCES: Author calculations using 2016–2017 Common Core data obtained via the National Center for Education Statistics' Elementary/Secondary Information System (U.S. Department of Education, National Center for Education Statistics, undated). The data in that system are from U.S. Department of Education, National Center for Education Statistics, Common Core of Data (CCD), 2017a, 2017b).

NOTE: Data are for school year 2016–2017.

The UPPI launched at a time of increased national focus on standards for principal preparation. In October 2015, a new set of national Professional Standards for Educational Leaders (PSEL) was approved (National Policy Board for Educational Administration, 2015).[5] The PSEL provided a set of research-based core principles and values about what constitutes effective school leadership. They can be used to inform policy and practice and to shape public understanding about what school leaders do (Smylie and Murphy, 2018). For example, Standard 1: Mission, Vision and Core Values specifies that "Effective educational leaders develop, advocate, and enact a shared mission, vision, and core values of high-quality education and academic success and well-being of each student" (National Policy Board for Educational Administration, 2015, p. 9). As part of UPPI, teams were explicitly asked to evaluate how well state and program standards align with the PSEL. The complementary National Educational Leadership Preparation (NELP) standards (University Council for Educational Administration, 2018) were available for preparation programs to use beginning in January 2018. The NELP standards apply the PSEL specifically to novice administrators and preparation program graduates. They provide a basis for principal preparation program accreditation.

Changes at the federal level also had implications for state policy. The Every Student Succeeds Act (ESSA; Pub. L. 114-95, 2015)—a reauthorization of the federal Elementary and Secondary Education Act (Pub. L. 89-10, 1965)—was passed in 2015. ESSA is notable for two reasons relevant to this report. First, it provides opportunities for states to use federal funds to pursue initiatives—including enhancing principal preparation programs—that will improve the quality and effectiveness of principals and other school leaders (Herman et al., 2017). Second, relative to the No Child Left Behind Act (Pub. L. 107-110, 2002) that it replaced, ESSA returns authority for a range of education policy issues to states and local education agencies. ESSA also explicitly requires states to consult with specific stakeholder groups on the development of the ESSA plan and other decisions (Council of Chief State School Officers, 2020).

## State Policy Levers to Influence Principal Quality

What is the potential scope of state action to improve principal quality? In this report, we focus on seven policy levers that states can use to improve school leadership. The first six of these were described by Manna (2015):

- setting principal standards
- recruiting aspiring principals into the profession

[5] The National Policy Board for Educational Administration is an organizational alliance created to advance school leadership through research, policy, and practice activities. Member organizations include the Council of Chief State School Officers, the International Council of Professors of Educational Leadership, the National Association of Elementary and School Principals, the National Association of Secondary School Principals, the American Association of School Administrators, and the University Council for Educational Administration (UCEA). UCEA is a member organization of higher education institutions with programs in education leadership and policy and their professors.

- licensing new and veteran principals
- approving and overseeing principal preparation programs
- supporting principals' growth with professional development
- evaluating principals.

We also consider the additional lever:

- using leader tracking systems to support analysis of aspiring and established school leaders' experiences and outcomes as they progress along the pathway from teacher to principal and beyond (Grissom, Mitani, and Woo, 2019).

Table 1.2 summarizes key policy actions associated with each lever. We elaborate on the policy levers and actions below, drawing on the Manna (2015) framework and other literature to highlight what is known about effective and prevalent practices across states.

### Standards

State principal standards establish common expectations about the knowledge, skills, abilities, and dispositions required of anyone who serves as a principal in the state. These standards help align the perspectives and actions of a variety of stakeholders, including principals, aspiring principals, preparation programs, superintendents, professional development providers, and state officials. Manna (2015) recommends that

**Table 1.2**
**Overview of Key Policy Actions, by Policy Lever**

| Policy Lever | Key Actions |
|---|---|
| Standards | • Adopt state standards for school principals<br>• Promote the use of state standards |
| Recruitment of aspiring leaders | • Establish prerequisites for program participation<br>• Subsidize participation in pre-service programs<br>• Encourage effective program recruitment practice |
| Licensure | • Determine licensure pathways<br>• Determine licensure requirements |
| Program approval and oversight | • Determine types of providers that can offer programs<br>• Establish criteria for program approval/renewal<br>• Approve programs<br>• Specify program content/structure |
| Professional development | • Establish requirements for principal professional development<br>• Support or offer principal professional development |
| Evaluation | • Establish content criteria<br>• Establish process expectations<br>• Establish reporting requirements |
| Leader tracking systems | • Support data systems for tracking aspiring and current principals |

states develop standards specifically for principals as opposed to school administrators more generally.

According to a review done by the Education Commission of the States in 2018, all states, including UPPI states, have leader standards (Scott, 2018). Further, 48 states have adopted leader standards that are consistent with national, research-based standards for principals. These leader standards include either the PSEL released in 2015 (National Policy Board for Educational Administration, 2015) or the earlier 2008 version of the standard (National Conference of State Legislatures, 2020). These standards articulate goals for school leader practice in activities ranging from setting mission, vision, and core values to creating conditions that ensure equity to supporting a professional community for teachers and staff.

Manna (2015) notes that developing standards is only a first step to influencing the quality of school leadership. The full power of standards is realized when they are *put to use* through other levers (Manna, 2015; Smylie and Murphy, 2018). For example, states can use standards to guide principal preparation programs to focus on critical leadership knowledge, skills, and dispositions (Smylie and Murphy, 2018). We will discuss this indirect and pervasive mechanism of influence for leadership standards further in Chapter Three.

#### Recruitment of Aspiring Leaders

State leaders can help build the pool of diverse, qualified principals by promoting recruitment and selection practices that draw the strongest candidates into preparation programs. Prior research suggests that states can influence recruitment by promoting specific approaches for programs to use in recruiting and selecting candidates (such as collaboration with districts); encouraging programs to systematically and proactively recruit candidates who would broaden the pipeline; altering incentives to draw desirable candidates into the pool; encouraging programs to use application criteria that measure qualities needed for on-the-job performance (e.g., success as a teacher improving student achievement, performance on an assessment of dispositions); and supporting data and analyses to forecast future principal workforce needs (Manna, 2015; Anderson and Reynolds, 2015a).

#### Licensure

Principal licensure authorizes individuals to practice as a principal in the state (Professional Educator Standards Boards Association, 2017). Manna (2015, p. 33) describes licensure as "the state's key power" when it comes to school principals. Davis (2016) highlights licensure along with program approval as "two particularly strong" (p. 14) policy levers available to states and recommends that states consider improving the alignment between licensure requirements and on-the-job responsibilities of principals. A survey of superintendents described in Davis (2016) suggested that most superintendents perceive that states are not effectively leveraging their authority with regard to licensure and program oversight.

States make several policy choices concerning principal licensure that can have implications for principal quality. One is **defining the scope of the license** that principals are required to hold. States can choose to offer a broad license that applies to all school administration positions (assistant principals, principals, nurse supervisors, district central office staff, and superintendents), or states can target licensure more specifically to school building administration positions or to the principalship specifically. Aspiring leaders may prefer a broader license, as it offers more flexibility and access to job options. But Manna (2015) argues that having a general license that includes principals with other job categories can obscure the unique role and contributions of school principals. He argues for standards, preparation programs, and licensure requirements that differentiate among roles and focus specifically on principals.

States also must decide whether to require **assessments** as part of the licensure process and, if so, how to implement that requirement. Thirty-six states require candidates to pass an assessment of some kind to earn their licenses (Anderson and Reynolds, 2015a). Types of assessments used by states for this purpose are portfolio review (e.g., submitting examples of one's work), performance-based assessments (e.g., completing job-like tasks), and standardized tests. Anderson and Reynolds (2015a) suggests that portfolio review or performance-based assessment may be a more holistic and accurate approach to measuring candidate competence, but found that only six states nationally required the use of a performance-based assessment or portfolio review.[6] Standardized assessments are more common and offer some advantages but also raise some issues. While standardized assessments may help ensure that candidates have a minimum level of skills and knowledge necessary to be successful school leaders, performance on standardized assessments is not necessarily a strong predictor of candidate success on the job (Grissom, Mitani, and Blissett, 2017) and may be subject to biases that unfairly disadvantage certain candidates. Such limitations may be due to the implementation of an assessment requirement rather than the requirement itself. The value of standardized assessments could be enhanced by identifying those assessments that are aligned to state standards and that best allow candidates to demonstrate skills and abilities that are most needed on the job.

Two other common requirements for principal certification are **teaching experience** and **advanced degrees**. Prior research and expert opinion suggest that principals need some teaching experience to be effective instructional leaders at their schools (Anderson and Reynolds, 2015a). However, a meta-analysis of research on the relationship between principal behaviors and outcomes finds that behaviors that draw on

---

[6] For performance-based review, the candidate demonstrates the ability to carry out a job task, under observation. For a portfolio review, the candidate assembles examples of his or her work throughout the course or program.

nonteaching skills, such as organizational management and administration, may be just as important to outcomes (Liebowitz and Porter, 2019). As a result, states must carefully weigh the emphasis placed on teaching experience. Anderson and Reynolds (2015a) also recommend that states require an advanced degree in the area of education administration or another related field to promote the quality of principal preparation, although there is not yet strong evidence supporting that recommendation. Anderson and Reynolds (2015a) found that slightly less than half of states in the nation require a master's degree in educational leadership or a related field.

### Program Approval and Oversight

Because all states have a pathway to the principalship that involves participation in a state-approved program, state actions related to program approval and oversight have significant potential to influence the quality of school leadership across the state (Manna, 2015). Manna recommends that states actively engage in program oversight and create incentives for quality improvement but also allow for program flexibility and innovation.

In all states, an arm of the state department of education or other state-level education agency is involved in the program approval process. That might be an independent or semi-independent professional standards board, the state board of education, or another division within the department of education. Some states also turn to the Council for the Accreditation of Educator Preparation (CAEP), a national-level organization, for accreditation. CAEP is a national educator preparation program accreditor that reviews colleges of education and specific programs within them. CAEP uses the NELP standards to review education leadership preparation programs. Some states allow the CAEP review to count for the state program approval process, and others use it in parallel with the state process.[7] The options are defined by the state's agreement with CAEP (CAEP, 2019b).

State policy determines what **types of providers** can be authorized to offer state-approved principal preparation programs that meet licensure requirements. All states authorize, at minimum, institutions of higher education to serve as providers. Some states also authorize alternative providers such as districts, county offices, charter organizations, and third-party organizations, such as professional associations.

States can require preparation programs to incorporate certain **content, processes, or practices** as a condition of state approval. For example, some states require programs to develop partnerships with the districts that employ their graduates.[8] This

---

7 Among the seven UPPI states, six states (California, Connecticut, Georgia, Kentucky, North Carolina, and Virginia) have state partnership agreements with CAEP that extend beyond oversight of leader preparation programs to also include oversight of education preparation programs in general.

8 UCEA (2015) notes that components of an effective university-district partnership include "district-provider collaboration on selection," "alignment between district needs and program needs," and a "commitment from district to provide a clinically rich internship experience."

practice can benefit districts by providing them with candidates who are trained to meet their specific needs, and by creating a "more committed leadership pool" (Darling-Hammond, Hyler, and Gardner, 2017).

In recent years, states have focused attention on specifying parameters for or characteristics of the **clinical experience** component of the principal preparation program. Research points to six criteria associated with effective clinical experiences (Anderson and Reynolds, 2015a):

- "Deliberately structured"
- "Field work that is tightly integrated with curriculum"
- "Engagement in core leadership responsibilities"
- "Supervision by an expert veteran"
- "Exposure to multiple sites and/or diverse populations"
- "300+ hours of field-based experiences."

Although Anderson and Reynolds (2015a) suggests that states should consider requiring programs to meet at least three of the above criteria, Manna (2015) argues that highly specific program requirements can be a barrier to innovation.

In addition to having program requirements on the books, states also make choices about how they **oversee** adherence to the requirements. While there is little research exploring the impact of state oversight of principal preparation programs, Anderson and Reynolds (2015b) argue that oversight is necessary to ensure the program approval requirements are met in practice. They suggest the following criteria for effective state oversight: use of an oversight plan and timeline, documentation, an experienced and trained oversight team, and feedback mechanisms.

### Professional Development

Supporting high-quality principal professional development has been a relatively overlooked state policy lever, as professional development is generally viewed as the responsibility of principals and districts that employ them. A national survey revealed that while nearly all principals reported receiving some professional development in the past year, the format and perceived value of that support varied widely (Johnston, Kaufman, and Thomson, 2016), mirroring findings about teacher professional development (TNTP, 2015). States could play a role in promoting access to high-quality professional development by encouraging participation in ongoing professional development (e.g., through licensure renewal requirements) and providing information or resources to direct principals toward higher-quality professional development options.

Although limited rigorous evidence exists, there is consensus among researchers and professional learning advocates on some features of high-quality professional learning for principals (Chiang et al., 2016; Herman et al., 2017; Learning Forward, 2011; Rowland, 2017; Turnbull, Riley, and MacFarlane, 2013). Most critical is that the learning be tailored to the needs of principals, occur within learning communities, involve on-the-job experiences, and be continuous rather than consisting of isolated activities (Chiang et al., 2016; Herman et al., 2017; Learning Forward, 2011; Rowland, 2017; Turnbull, Riley, and MacFarlane, 2013). Coaching and mentoring are identified as promising approaches, even beyond the novice phase of a principal's career (Herman et al., 2017; Chiang et al., 2016; Rowland, 2017). High-quality professional learning should focus on content prioritized in the PSEL for what principals should know and be able to do (Rowland, 2017). These features are similar to those that have been associated with high-quality teacher professional development (Darling-Hammond, Hyler, and Gardner, 2017).

Anderson and Reynolds (2015a) found that 45 states, including all the UPPI states, have a continuing education or professional development requirement for credentialed principals, such as credit hours or professional development plans. However, only 15 of the 45 met "strong" professional development requirements; "strong" requirements, according to Anderson and Reynolds (2015a), are activities tailored to practicing principals or based on job performance, while weak requirements tend to focus on the number of credit hours.

### Evaluation

Although principal evaluation is a core responsibility of districts, states can influence district practice by clearly defining expectations for the principal evaluation process and supporting the evaluation with state-approved standards and rigorous tools or rubrics (Shelton, 2013; Fuller, Hollingworth, and Lui, 2015). In other words, state evaluation systems can specify parameters for the evaluation process districts should follow, the content of the evaluation, or both. Process requirements or guidance might specify the frequency of the evaluation, who is eligible to conduct the evaluation, or how evaluation results are used to inform district decisions. Content requirements or guidance might require or recommend alignment of evaluation metrics to standards, use of a specific evaluation rubric, or consideration of student achievement growth in principal evaluations.

A review of state (plus District of Columbia) principal evaluation system requirements identified the following common state approaches (number of states with the requirement in place in parenthesis): required use of student growth data in evaluation (34), required annual evaluations for all principals (30), required or optional use of survey data in evaluation (31), required annual observations to inform evaluation (28), and required development of a plan to support struggling principals (24). The review found that, between 2015 and 2019, more states were stepping back from evaluation requirements rather than advancing them (National Center for Teacher Quality, 2019).

Prior research points to pervasive limitations of principal evaluation, suggesting that it is an area worthy of more state-level attention. For example, Clifford and Ross (2011) found that principals view evaluations as cursory and routine, even if the tools themselves are useful, and that evaluations are inconsistent, indicating that performance measures are not aligned with state or national standards. Shelton (2013) found that several state evaluations are not aligned with quality performance standards, and the majority of evaluations do not include valid or reliable methods.

### Leader Tracking Systems

Leader tracking systems are designed to capture longitudinal data about the characteristics, experiences, and outcomes of aspiring and current school leaders. These individual-level records help in identifying potential candidates for preparation programs, matching leaders with positions, and supporting tailored professional development. Further, they can help preparation programs evaluate the impact of their programs by looking at their graduates' outcomes and help state officials evaluate the success of particular preparation programs.

Although Manna (2015) does not identify leader tracking systems as a standalone policy lever, his report does include several data-related recommendations that could be supported through leader tracking systems: forecasting future trends in principal vacancies to inform recruitment priorities, serving as an information clearinghouse on preparation program offerings and quality, and tapping workforce data to identify recently retired principals who could mentor novice principals in the state. Fulfilling these objectives would require access to and integration of data from districts and preparation programs across the state.

Principal preparation programs can use leader tracking system data on their graduates to improve their programs. Chiang et al. (2016) highlights the importance of tracking a range of outcomes for those who complete principal preparation programs. Grissom, Mitani, and Woo (2019) describe heightened interest among states in linking program graduates to on-the-job outcomes and holding them accountable for those outcomes. The authors leverage data efforts undertaken by Tennessee to analyze the relationship between principal preparation programs and licensure examination scores and failure rates, placement as a principal or assistant principal in Tennessee and retention in those roles, and different performance evaluation metrics. The Danforth Education Leadership Program at the University of Washington gives a performance guarantee to districts hiring its graduates.

The Ohio State Department of Higher Education links data from the Ohio Department of Education to data from institutions of higher education to create a range of metrics of interest to aspiring administrators, districts, and administrator preparation programs, as well as the state. For example, the system relates preparation programs to Ohio Principal Evaluation System data, licensure examination results, placement, and principal value-added information (Chiang et al., 2016).

## Methods Overview

### Data Sources

We used three key data sources for this study. First, we drew on data collected from seven rounds of visits to UPPI sites, conducted in spring and fall from 2017 to 2019, and spring 2020. We conducted a total of 49 site visits across the seven UPPI sites. As part of the site visits, we conducted hour-long interviews with the university-based lead at the UPPI site (n = 51 total over seven site visits) and the lead(s) at the state partner institution (n = 54 total over seven site visits).

Second, between April and July 2019, we conducted 47 additional interviews with state-level stakeholders across the seven UPPI states. We conducted the 45- to 60-minute interviews by phone or, when possible, in person during our spring 2019 site visits. Interviewees were identified using a snowball sampling method that included recommendations from UPPI university-based and state partner leads. Interviewees spanned six main roles: representatives from state government (n = 4 across seven states); state department of education or professional standards boards, beyond UPPI state leads (n = 6); educational cooperatives or county offices (n = 6); districts or related associations (n = 15); university faculty or administrators, beyond UPPI university-based leads (n = 8); and not-for-profit or advocacy organizations (n = 8). We asked interviewees about the agenda status of school leader preparation in the state and the extent to which they agreed that their state uses each of the seven policy levers we were interested in to influence the quality of school leadership effectively. Table 1.3 summarizes the interview data collected for this report.

Third, we reviewed relevant secondary data, such as state ESSA plans, state licensure requirements, state legislation, reports from state departments of education and professional standards boards about the policy levers, and research literature on school leadership.

We provide more information on our data sources in Appendix A.

### Data Analysis

We generated detailed notes or transcriptions of all interview data, then coded and analyzed these in Dedoose (Dedoose, 2018), a cross-platform internet application that assists with qualitative data. The state profiles in Appendix B are based on publicly available information and aggregate (unidentifiable) characterizations drawn from primary qualitative data collection by the RAND team. The profiles serve as case studies in this report. For more information about data analysis, including a discussion of the limitations, see Appendix A.

**Table 1.3**
**Interviews That Informed This Analysis**

| | Number of Interviews | | | |
|---|---|---|---|---|
| State (UPPI University) | With UPPI University-Based Leads (Spring and Fall 2017–2019 and Spring 2020) | With UPPI State Partner Leads (Spring and Fall 2017–2019 and Spring 2020) | With Additional Stakeholders (April–July 2019) | Total |
| California (San Diego State University) | 7 | 7 | 12 | 26 |
| Connecticut (University of Connecticut) | 7 | 10 | 3 | 20 |
| Florida (Florida Atlantic University) | 7 | 10 | 5 | 22 |
| Georgia (Albany State University) | 7 | 8 | 4 | 19 |
| Kentucky (Western Kentucky University) | 7 | 7 | 8 | 22 |
| North Carolina (North Carolina State University) | 9 | 7 | 10 | 26 |
| Virginia (Virginia State University) | 7 | 5 | 5 | 17 |
| Total | 51 | 54 | 47 | 152 |

## Organization of This Report

The remainder of this report consists of five chapters:

- Chapter Two identifies some features of the context that have implications for policy lever use and policy change.
- Chapter Three describes how each lever is used and provides examples of policy change affecting the levers.
- Chapter Four presents cross-cutting themes about how the levers are used, including how the levers operate (e.g., who is influenced by the lever and how they are influenced), how different levers are interconnected, and which factors stakeholders perceive as contributing to effective use.
- Chapter Five discusses the facilitators of and barriers to policy change.
- Chapter Six highlights some key findings and offers recommendations.

In the appendixes, we provide additional information about our methods and present a detailed, coherent profile for each state, addressing the state context, the agenda status of school leadership, and the use of each policy lever.

CHAPTER TWO

# State Context for School Leadership Policy

In this chapter, we address our first research question by focusing on the context in which state policy levers are used to influence principal quality. We begin by describing the key actors in state policy regarding principal quality and the roles they play. Then we revisit the pathway to the principalship presented in Figure 1.1, emphasizing important points of variation relevant to our later discussion about how states use the seven key policy levers.

## State Policy Actors That Influence Principal Quality

Our review of state policy efforts confirms findings from prior research that state policy to improve principal quality involves multiple actors, sometimes conflicting policy agendas, and a wide array of strategies for shaping policy (Kingdon, 1984; Manna, 2015). In Table 2.1, we summarize the key actors and their roles, delineating common categories of actors across states and roles or functions that are important to school leadership issues (the light red boxes signify primary responsibilities).

Three roles are especially important to the use of state-level policy to improve principal quality: setting direction through legislation and funding, shaping the direction more precisely through regulation and oversight, and providing resources and services. Although there are clear formal leaders for each role (e.g., the legislature is responsible for developing legislation), a wide array of stakeholders is involved informally in each role. For example, the governor, department of education, professional educator standards board, and nonstate entities influence the direction of legislation. In some states, the legislature is a powerful force in setting policy, writing specific and directive legislation. In some states, governors play a strong role in influencing school leadership policy through appointments, initiatives, or executive orders. Below, we highlight some insights about the state policy context that are relevant for efforts to improve principal quality.

**Table 2.1**
**Overview of Key Actors and Roles in State Principal Policy**

| | Roles | | |
|---|---|---|---|
| **Key Actors** | **Legislation and Funding** | **Regulations and Oversight** | **Resources and Services** |
| Governor | • Approves legislation, budget | • Appoints leaders and commissions to shape policy | • Provides information and professional development<br>• Supports or promotes collaboration |
| State legislature | • Develops, approves legislation | | |
| State department of education[a] | • Provides input on legislation, budget | • Develops regulations<br>• Establishes licensure standards and program approval requirements<br>• Grants licenses<br>• Oversees programs | • Provides information and professional development<br>• Supports or promotes collaboration |
| Cooperatives or county offices | | | • Provide districts with support for principal preparation, hiring, and professional development<br>• Support or promote collaboration |
| Professional educator standards board | | • Establishes licensure standards and program approval requirements<br>• Grants licenses<br>• Oversees programs | |
| Nonstate entities[b] | • Advise on legislation, budget | • Advise on regulations | • Provide information and professional development<br>• Support or promote collaboration |

NOTE: The light red boxes signify primary responsibilities.

[a] Includes the state superintendents and state boards of education, as well as offices within the department of education such as offices for accountability, standards, and licensure.

[b] For example, professional associations, foundations, nonprofits, and institutions of higher education.

### Legislatures vary in their degree of involvement in principal quality issues

State legislatures typically shape statewide principal policy through legislation and appropriation of funds. Some legislatures are more hands-off, delegating details of principal preparation policymaking to state departments of education or professional standards boards. In contrast, other legislatures have crafted highly specific laws, leaving little flexibility for the department of education to further shape policy direction. Interviewees reported that, in these cases, the roles of the state department of education and other stakeholders in setting policy related to principal quality can be somewhat bounded by the legislature.

### In states with professional standards boards, those boards have substantial influence over licensing and program approval

The responsibility for licensing administrators and approving preparation programs generally falls to the state department of education. However, in some states, professional educator standards boards take on this role. Nationally, 15 states have independent or semi-independent professional standards boards, including the UPPI states of California, Georgia, and Kentucky (National Association of State Directors of Teacher Education and Certification, 2019). As of 2017, an additional 14 states had advisory (not independent) professional standards boards, including UPPI states Florida and Virginia (Professional Educator Standards Boards Association, 2017); North Carolina launched its Professional Educator Preparation and Standards Commission in late 2017 (Bell, 2017). Connecticut does not appear to have a professional standards board (Connecticut Education Association, 2011; Professional Educator Standards Boards Association, 2017). In states where they exist (see Box 2.1), professional standards boards can provide a locus of expertise on school leadership issues that may not be available in the state department of education. However, communication between the professional educator standards boards and departments of education is essential when the responsibilities are shared (National Association of State Directors of Teacher Education and Certification, 2019). We found that, in states with an independent professional educator standards board, the board had substantial power within its scope of responsibility. The legislation authorizing such boards calls for broad stakeholder representation, which, in turn, can expand their capacity and support.

### Some states delegate support efforts to regional entities

State departments of education provide direct services to schools and districts, such as statewide professional development or principal coaching. In addition, regional cooperatives and county offices exist in some, but not all, of the states in our study. Box 2.2 describes such entities in Georgia. Where they exist, they play a key role in providing services such as principal professional development, especially in small or rural districts. In some states, these entities may

**Box 2.1**
**California Commission on Teacher Credentialing**

The California Commission on Teacher Credentialing is responsible for developing policies and regulations for teacher and principal preparation and certification, as well as accrediting educator preparation programs. The governor appoints 14 of the 15 commissioners and the state superintendent appoints the 15th. In addition, higher education groups—independent colleges and universities, the University of California, California State University, and California Community Colleges—each have a nonvoting representative on the commission.

**Box 2.2**
**Georgia's Regional Educational Service Agencies**

In Georgia, Regional Educational Service Agencies offer a wide range of resources and services to school leaders and potential leaders, including leadership development seminars, conferences, classes, access to resource libraries and support in developing leadership teams. They are funded by the state and governed by local boards.

**Box 2.3**
**North Carolina's Nongovernmental Organizations Promote Principal Preparation**

In North Carolina, nongovernmental organizations are deeply engaged in principal preparation policy. Three professional associations—the North Carolina Alliance for School Leadership Development, the North Carolina Principal and Assistant Principal Association, and the North Carolina Administrator and Superintendent Association—work closely together to convene state education leaders; inform legislative and policy priorities; provide direct supports, such as principal professional development; and manage state-funded programs. For example, the North Carolina Principal and Assistant Principal Association provides the main professional development opportunities in the state, and the closely related North Carolina Alliance for School Leadership Development administers a state grant program to support principal preparation. Three nonprofit organizations—the Belk Foundation, Business for Educational Success and Transformation (BEST NC), and the Hunt Institute—also promote principal preparation. BEST NC spent a year interviewing stakeholders before deciding to focus on principals. BEST NC advocated successfully for the state's Transforming Principal Preparation Program, which supports preparation program improvement, and worked closely with the state to address principal pay issues.

offer state-approved preparation or professional development programs.

### Many informal actors influence state policy on principal quality

In all seven states, there are a wide range of nongovernmental organizations that influence school leadership policy by informing legislation, advising on implementation, and serving on task forces and panels. Box 2.3 provides a concrete example from North Carolina. In most of the seven states, professional associations (e.g., principal associations and sometimes faculty, superintendent, or school board associations) engage in principal preparation policy. In several states, higher education councils or university systems work closely with the state department of education around principal preparation policy. Nonprofit organizations also engage in policy, sometimes using independent resources to promote policy priorities. Influence on principal quality appears to be greater when organizations have expertise, but the power of individual personalities and connections is not trivial.

### Features of the governance structure may influence policy alignment and stability

Most states have a state board of education and a chief state school officer (often called the state superintendent). In most states, the governor appoints members of the board of education, and either the governor or the state board appoints the chief state school officer. Although the terms of board members do not always coincide with the term of the governor, turnover in the governor's office can lead to changes among those responsible for education policy. In 11 states, including three UPPI states, the chief state school officer is directly elected (National Association of State Boards of Education, 2020). Governance structures that provide for separate election of the chief state school officer could promote broader or conflicting perspectives within a state's education policy leadership, as voters may elect superintendents whose views do not necessarily align with the governor's. Because legislators and other elected officials potentially play a role in school leadership policy in all states, there is the potential for significant shifts in direction each election cycle—a challenge raised by interviewees.

**Few stakeholders identified school leadership as a top state education priority but did not view this as a problem**

Manna (2015) found that principals have low agenda status, meaning that state education policy agendas prioritize other topics over principals. He argues that this low agenda status is a barrier to improvements in principal quality and recommends that states work to "move principals higher on the state policy agenda" (Manna, 2015, p. 12). Consistent with Manna's findings, stakeholders we interviewed did not often mention school leadership as a top education priority for the state. School leadership was mentioned only four times in 47 interviews. While school leadership was not often mentioned, many of the issues that were identified as top priorities hinge on quality school leadership (e.g., school safety, student achievement/closing gaps, school improvement, equity). Some of our interviewees recognized that the problem (and solution) underlying many of these issues is school leadership. However, they did not believe that their state generally positioned broader initiatives around school leadership.

In spite of this low agenda status, all seven UPPI states mentioned school leadership in their ESSA plan, and two of them (California, North Carolina) opted to set aside 3 percent of their Title II, Part A, funds for school leadership (New Leaders, 2018).

Stakeholders generally did not frame low agenda status of school leadership as a problem. They reasoned that with lower priority comes less scrutiny and controversy, and so those working on school leadership can proceed steadily and focus on foundational issues. Many interviewees reported advantages to embedding school leadership within various key agenda topics (school improvement, equity, etc.).

## Variation Across States in the Pathway to the Principalship

Our research revealed that the pathway to the principalship varies across states. Drawing on interview data and descriptive, publicly available documents, we mapped the basic pathway through which teachers become principals in UPPI states (see Figure 2.1). This figure highlights two key dimensions of variation that have potential implications for the use of policy levers: additional stages of licensure and alternative pathways in addition to the pathway through state-approved preparation programs.

#### Some states have multiple stages of licensure

Two UPPI states (North Carolina and Virginia) have a one-stage process for principal licensure. The other states have a multi-stage process.[1] Individuals in California, Connecticut, and Kentucky can serve as a principal after completing the first stage of the process with some restrictions, conditions, or requirements. In Georgia, individuals are allowed to act as an assistant principal after the first stage but must complete the second stage to act as a principal. In Florida, the state only requires individuals to complete the first stage in order to serve as a principal but the employing district can require completion of the second stage. Figure 2.1 reflects the possibility of a second stage of the pathway to the principalship.

Research suggests that the multi-staged licensure structure can be used by states to craft differentiated program requirements that (1) prepare novice administrators for their first administrative job and then (2) give novice administrators the opportunity to develop their skills while on the job (Anderson and Reynolds, 2015a). When activating the program approval lever for the second stage, states have the opportunity to set requirements around the components of principal induction that have been found to be important, such as the selection of mentors, the types of professional development opportunities provided, or the duration of induction (Hitt, Tucker, and Young, 2012).

#### Some states offer alternative pathways that bypass a state-approved program

All UPPI states have licensure pathways that involve completing a state-approved preparation program. Three states have alternative pathways that allow candidates who do not already hold a principal certification to bypass the program pathway.[2] Virginia's alternative pathway is available to individuals who hold a master's degree. Virginia requires additional graduate coursework and preparation along with the recommendation of the superintendent in the district employing the candidate. California's alternative pathway allows candidates to bypass the first stage of the two-stage licensure process by passing an assessment. Kentucky's alternative pathway allows individuals to obtain a provisional certificate based on demonstrated proficiency through a process overseen by authorized principal preparation programs. In addition, all UPPI

---

[1] Generally, in states with a multi-staged structure, there are two stages: a provisional license allowing the graduate to serve as assistant principal, and a full principal license. Connecticut uses a three-stage process. In all but one state, graduates can technically step into the principal position after completing the first stage of the process, if only on a provisional basis. States use different terminology (e.g. *level*, *tier*, or descriptive terms) to refer to the stages. In the main text, we use the term *stage*. In the Appendix B profiles, we use each state's terminology.

[2] Several states approve different categories of programs and refer to one or more of these categories as *alternative*. We do not consider these to be alternative pathways as they still involve completion of a state-approved program and hence do not bypass the program requirement.

**Figure 2.1**
**Some States Have a Multi-Staged Program Pathway and/or an Alternative Pathway to the Principalship**

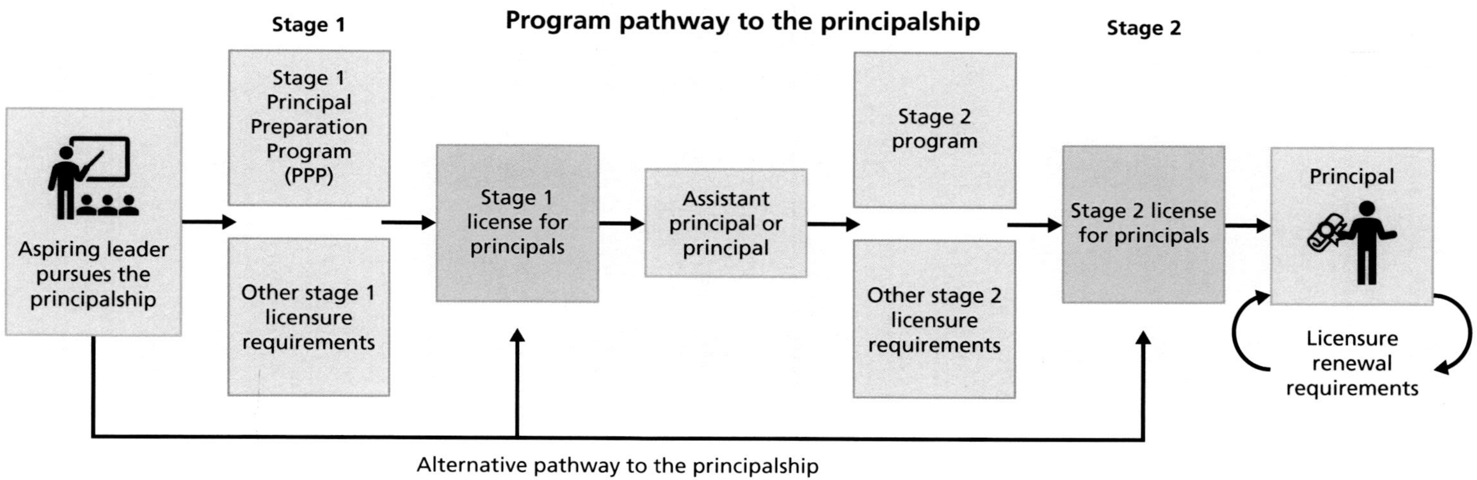

states have streamlined licensure processes for individuals who already hold a principal license in another state. These processes account for equivalent experience or preparation obtained in another state (Scott, 2018). Many states also have streamlined pathways for special populations such as military veterans. We do not consider these streamlined procedures to be alternative pathways. UCEA, which is a member organization for university-based preparation programs, expressed some skepticism about the ability of such alternative, non-program-based pathways to support principal quality (Anderson and Reynolds, 2015a). Our review of the legislation creating alternative pathways to licensure indicates that the rationale lies in the perceived need for flexibility at the district level to address school leader shortages and to provide an option for aspiring principals who have career experiences outside of education.

Having described some key features of the context that influence use of policy levers in UPPI states, we turn in Chapter Three to a lever-by-lever description of the use of levers and resulting policy changes in these states.

CHAPTER THREE

# How UPPI States Use Policy Levers

In this chapter, we address our second research question, focusing on the policy levers that states are using and the ways in which they are using them, as well as policy changes states have made that can affect the way levers are used. The findings we present in the chapter are descriptive in nature and lay the groundwork for a discussion of cross-cutting themes in later chapters of the report. Readers who are more interested in those themes may choose to skip this chapter. Given the small sample size, we are unable to provide sweeping explanations for the variation we observe; however, we expect our descriptive findings to be helpful to other states in part because they are drawn from states that were considered to have a favorable state context for school leadership. This description is based on our analysis of documents and interviews. Throughout, we use quantifiers to provide a sense of the prevalence of the activity, idea, or policy among UPPI states. We use *few* or *some* to indicate fewer than half (i.e., 1–3 of the states); *most* to indicate more than half (i.e., 4–6 of the states); and *all* to mean all (i.e., 7 out of the 7 UPPI states). In discussing examples of policy change, we focus on changes made since 2016 to improve the quality of school leadership. Many of the changes featured in this chapter were in progress or initiated prior to the launch of UPPI; therefore, the activities should not be interpreted as stemming from UPPI, except where explicitly noted. The chapter concludes with some discussion of how the levers exert influence on principal quality.

## Standards

### How the Standards Lever Is Used

All UPPI states have principal or leadership standards and have updated their standards since 2011. Most states have standards that are aligned to either the Professional Standards for Educational Leaders (PSEL) or its predecessor, the Interstate School Leaders Licensure Consortium depending on when the last update occurred).

All the UPPI states actively use the standards in some way. All states communicate their standards, making them visible to the public, districts, and other stakeholders. Sometimes nonstate actors, such as nonprofits, play a role in developing and providing resources around these standards. For example, in California, the leadership standards were drafted with the input of various stakeholders, including representatives from the association of school administrators, nonprofit organizations, public and private universities, and county offices of education. In all states, the standards provide the foundation for licensure; states that require candidates to pass a licensure assessment align their assessments to standards. States also actively use the standards in preparation program approval and in evaluation.

### Examples of Recent Policy Changes Related to Standards

Between 2016 and 2018, three UPPI states adopted or updated their leadership standards. California revised leadership standards for novice administrators. Meanwhile, Georgia and Kentucky formally adopted (or adapted with minor revisions) the national PSEL as their state standard for guiding the development and practice of educational leaders. In these states, the efforts were led by the professional standards board or commissions with input from a wide range of stakeholders (see Box 3.1). These efforts took a year or more to implement. Other states may adopt or align current standards to the PSEL in the future.

As illustrated in sections below, the revision of standards in Georgia and Kentucky led to changes in other arenas, including program approval, licensure, and/or the evaluation of principals. In this respect, the standards revision was a critical policy change in these states. In California, changes in licensure prompted a revision of standards materials to ensure consistency and alignment with recently revised state leader standards (see Box 3.2).

**Box 3.1.**
**Georgia Adopted and Adapted PSEL to Align with National Standards**

In Georgia, the state's professional standards commission (PSC) adopted a modified version of the PSEL as the state standards. Early in the UPPI effort, the state cross-walked the existing Georgia Education Leadership Standards (GELS) and the PSEL. This exercise revealed gaps, particularly with respect to equity, and helped the PSC realize the urgency of upgrading the state's standards. The PSC convened a task force that included program providers to tackle the work of revising the state standards. In September 2017, the PSC formally adopted an adapted version of the PSEL as the new GELS. The modifications involved tailoring the PSEL to the Georgia context. As of July 2018, Georgia educational leadership preparation program rules required all programs to align with the GELS.

## Recruitment

### How the Recruitment Lever Is Used

The recruitment lever includes state-level efforts to encourage the right number of people with the right backgrounds to enter principal preparation programs. As noted by Manna (2015), this is not simply about preparing "more" people but about encouraging those who really want to be administrators and have the capacity to be good administrators to enter the pathway. We observed two categories of recruitment policies in UPPI states. One was establishing requirements for program participants or how they are selected by programs. The other was providing support to aspiring leaders while they are in the pathway.

### *States establish requirements for entry into principal preparation programs*

All the UPPI states have program approval requirements related to candidate selection. For example, some states require those entering a principal preparation program to have teaching experience prior to program entry or upon graduation from the program, thereby limiting the pool of candidates to current of former teachers. Florida, in fact, requires program candidates to demonstrate instructional expertise and leadership potential, as reflected in performance evaluations, for admission into a stage 1 program. In Georgia, candidates for licensure must pass the Georgia Ethics for Educational Leadership Assessment prior to program entry (Georgia Professional Standards Commission, 2019).

Beyond prerequisites that candidates must satisfy, states also establish requirements for programs around candidate recruitment and selection. North Carolina, for example, obliges programs to "adopt rigorous selection criteria based on competencies that are predictive of success as a school leader," and lists several such criteria (North Carolina State Board of Education, 2018). Moreover, most UPPI states require principal preparation programs and school districts to work together for some part of the candidate selection process, such as recruitment, selection, or assessment of candidates.

**Box 3.2**
**California Revised Standards Materials in Response to Changes in Licensure and Accreditation**

In California, the state professional standards board has developed a portfolio of resources to help different groups apply the states standards for school administrators in their work.

The California Professional Standards for Education Leaders "identify what an administrator must know and be able to do to move into sustainable, effective practice. They are a set of broad policy standards that are the foundation for administrator preparation, induction, development, professional learning and evaluation in California" (California Commission on Teacher Credentialing [CTC], 2014, p. 1).

The California Administrator Performance Expectations describe the performance expectations for candidates in a first-stage credential program—when they are learning to become an administrator.

The California Administrator Content Expectations establish expectations about the content candidates need to know in order to meet the performance expectations. These are used by the professional standards board for program approval and oversight.

Efforts to overhaul licensure and accreditation led the state to revise the content and alignment of these three resources between 2016 and 2018. These updates have been led by the professional standards board with input from preparation program providers and other stakeholders.

***States offer programs incentivizing aspiring principals to enter the pipeline***

North Carolina (North Carolina State Education Assistance Authority, 1999) and Georgia (Georgia Governor's Office of Student Achievement, 2020a) influence recruitment and selection by providing direct support for candidates to participate in pre-service programs (see Boxes 3.3 and 3.4).

**Examples of Recent Policy Changes Related to Recruitment**

We identified few state-level change efforts since 2016 focused on the recruitment of aspiring school leaders. Those we noted involved the state providing funding and support to increase the number and improve the quality of aspiring school leaders without implementing requirements for all programs or candidates. One example of such a change concerns North Carolina's Principal Fellows Program (NC PFP) and its Transforming Principal Preparation Program (TP3). Effective June 2020, state legislation (SB 521) merged these two programs into a single funding source and program. A key purpose of this legislation is to improve alignment of the state's efforts to support programs and candidates in order to increase the number of high-quality principal candidates. (See Box 3.5.)

**Box 3.3**
**North Carolina Has Supported Promising Principal Candidates Since 1993**

North Carolina has supported promising principal candidates in completing a principal pre-service program through its North Carolina Principal Fellows Program (NC PFP). The program was created in 1993 by legislation enacted by the North Carolina General Assembly. Candidate selection for the program is guided by criteria established by legislation. These criteria included "evidence of effective leadership and management potential' and 'four years of successful teaching experience or relevant experience." Successful applicants receive a forgivable loan and a paid internship in a district in North Carolina. To be eligible for loan forgiveness, candidates are required to serve for four years as a school administrator at public school in the state. As discussed in Box 3.5, the NC PFP was recently combined with another program supporting preparation programs, with the new program still offering support directly to aspiring leaders.

## Licensure

### How the Licensure Lever Is Used

Through our review of approaches to licensure in UPPI states, we identified key state-level licensure policy choices: whether there is a license specific to the principalship, whether the state requires an assessment for licensure, and what other requirements candidates must meet for licensure. Below, we describe the range of approaches observed among UPPI states on each of these dimensions.

First, while all UPPI states require principals to have a license, none has a required license specific to principals alone. Although Manna (2015) highlights the benefits of a principal-specific license, our interviewees did not view the general administrative license as a significant barrier to promoting principal quality within their state. Inter-

**Box 3.4**
**Georgia's Governor's School Leadership Academy—Aspiring Principal Program**

The Governor's School Leadership Academy (GSLA) in Georgia was established by the governor in 2018 in partnership with state, regional, and local stakeholders. The GSLA provides pre-service leadership preparation to cohorts of aspiring principals and in-service support to cohorts of sitting principals. The GLSA launched its first Aspiring Principals cohort in school year 2018–19. The Aspiring Principals program offers participants a modest stipend and a range of professional development supports: in-person training, monthly meetings, one-on-one coaching, and job-embedded activities designed to help prepare aspiring principals for their first year on the job. Although successful completion of the Aspiring Principal Program does not lead to principal certification, the GSLA has established partnerships with universities and educator preparation program providers to share course credit and program requirements to ensure alignment among preparation programs.

**Box 3.5**
**North Carolina's New NC PFP Merges Funding from TP3 and the Original NC PFP to Support More-Qualified Principal Candidates**

The original NC Principal Fellows Program (NC PFP) was launched in 1993. It disbursed $3.2 million per year in forgivable scholarship loans to aspiring principals for one year of master's-level study at a participating institution, and a one-year paid internship in a district in North Carolina. The Transforming Principal Preparation Program (TP3), launched in 2015, was a competitive annual state grant valued at about $1 million. It was administered to North Carolina institutions of higher education—as opposed to individual students, in the case of the NC PFP. Programs applying for a TP3 grant must demonstrate how the program implemented research-based practices to support effective preparation of principals for high-needs schools. The TP3 was subsequently expanded and, as of the 2019–20 fiscal year, included $4.2 million in funding for six TP3 grantees (i.e., universities).

The original NC PFP and the TP3 merged their funding in June 2020. The combined program will be known as the NC Principal Fellows Program (NC PFP). In practice, principal preparation programs selected for the now six-year NC PFP grant program include the following features: (1) targeted efforts to recruit participants; (2) rigorous selection of participants; (3) implementation of a cohort model for a more supportive educational environment and a built-in professional network for graduates; (4) incorporation of professional leadership standards woven through all aspects of the program; (5) varied and frequent feedback from colleagues, faculty, mentors, and coaches; (6) an emphasis on inquiry-based, hands-on, and authentic learning experiences; (7) project-based learning methods and fieldwork to prepare participants to work in high-need communities and schools; (8) a full-time internship that allows participants to develop first-hand experience with the real responsibilities of the principalship; (9) collaborative partnerships with districts that inform the design of program features; and (10) continuous review and program improvement activities. Successful aspiring principals that apply to the program receive a forgivable loan, a ten-month paid internship, and assistance for books.

viewees did not think that licenses with a broader scope impeded efforts to promote principal quality because they saw the general administrator license as one focused on the principalship regardless. We observed ways in which states can prioritize the principalship within a more general administrative licensure structure by emphasizing the expectations for school principals in the licensure requirements (see Box 3.6).

Regarding assessments, with the exception of North Carolina, all UPPI states require candidates to pass at least one assessment to earn the license required to serve as a principal. For states that have a two-stage licensure process, the assessment typically occurs during the first stage, although Georgia requires assessments in both stages of licensure, and Florida is piloting a second-stage assessment. All the assessments are aligned to state standards or national standards.

There are some notable variations in format and content of assessments. Only two states require a portfolio review-type assessment in which candidates must complete various tasks during their clinical experience as well as submit evidence of their learning in various forms, such as videos, artifacts, student work, written narratives, agendas and minutes for meetings, and observation notes (Georgia Assessments for the Certification of Educators, 2020). Some non-portfolio-review assessments are more performance-based than others. They range from all selected response (i.e., multiple-choice) questions to assessments with a constructed-response (i.e., essay) section. For these, candidates may be asked to complete a "written performance assessment" by responding to scenarios or documents (Educational Testing Service, 2018a).

Table 3.1 summarizes the key features of the required assessments, highlighting that licensure assessment is an active area of state influence. It demonstrates that there is variation among the UPPI states in terms of how they approach licensure assessments, evidencing the array of assessment options available to state policymakers.

UPPI states have other requirements for licensure. This includes three or more years of teaching or other school-related experience, a master's degree (though not necessarily in educational leadership), and employment in an administrative role. In some states, requirements must be met before entering a preparation program, but in most cases, the licensure requirements can be achieved while a person is in a preparation program.

**Box 3.6**
**California's Performance Assessment Emphasizes the Skills Principals Need**

The California Administrator Performance Assessment provides one example of how states can emphasize the role of principals even though the administrative license allows holders to assume various administrative roles. The assessment has three components. The first focuses on "analyzing data to inform school improvement and promote equity." The second emphasizes "facilitating communities of practice," and the third focuses on "supporting teacher growth" (CTC, 2019a). All three components emphasize site leadership and the core skills required of building leaders.

**Table 3.1**
**Required Licensure Assessments, by State and Stage**

| State | Assessment | Format | Alignment to State or National Standards (PSEL) |
|---|---|---|---|
| California | California Administrator Performance Assessment (CalAPA) | • Performance assessment (portfolio documentation) | State |
| Connecticut | Educational Leadership: Administration and Supervision | • Selected-response<br>• Computer-based | National |
| Florida | Florida Educational Leadership Examination (FELE) | • Selected-response<br>• Written performance assessment<br>• Computer-based | State |
| Georgia | Georgia Assessments for the Certification of Educators (GACE) Educational Leadership assessment | • Selected-response<br>• Constructed-response<br>• Computer-based | State |
| | Performance Assessment for School Leaders (PASL) | • Performance assessment (portfolio documentation) | State |
| Kentucky | School Leaders Licensure Assessment (SLLA) | • Selected-response<br>• Constructed-response<br>• Computer-based | National |
| Virginia | School Leaders Licensure Assessment (SLLA) | • Selected-response<br>• Constructed-response<br>• Computer-based | National |

NOTES: All assessments in the table, except Georgia's Performance Assessment for School Leaders (PASL) occur during the first stage of the licensure process. As explained in the text, North Carolina is the only UPPI state that does not have a required assessment.

## Examples of Recent Policy Changes Related to Licensure

### *States delineated new licensure pathways*

Since 2016, some states have made or have been considering revisions to pathways leading to principal licensure. One type of revision, enacted in Georgia (see Box 3.7), helps ensure more comprehensive preparation for leadership positions at the principal level (and beyond). Another type of change aims to open the pipeline to more aspirants (see Box 3.8).

### *States adopted new licensure performance-based and/or standards-based assessments*

Most UPPI states have made or anticipate making changes to their licensure assessment. One particular trend is a shift toward performance-based assessments. In contrast to traditional knowledge-based assessments, these newer assessments are intended to assess the candidates' application of knowledge and skills related to school leadership in areas such as using and analyzing data for school improvement, developing con-

**Box 3.7**
**Georgia Instituted a Two-Stage Licensure Structure, Signaling Extended Preparation Needed for Leadership**

In 2016, the Georgia Professional Standards Commission instituted a two-stage structure with implications for licensure and for program approval. The first stage of licensure allows candidates to apply for school-level administrative positions below the principalship or district-level administrative positions not involving supervision of principals. The second stage of licensure is for those already in administrative positions (e.g., assistant principals) advancing to the principalship, the superintendency, and other administrative posts that involve the supervision of principals. Prior to this change, two licenses had been offered, but they distinguished between school-level leadership (which included roles such as teacher instructional leaders up to principalship) and district-level leadership. The new two-stage structure recognizes that aspiring principals need more training after they obtain their first-stage license.

**Box 3.8**
**Kentucky Reinterpreted Existing Regulation to Open Another Pathway to Licensure**

In Kentucky, a reinterpretation of an existing regulation meant that instead of progressing step-by-step through a principal preparation program, an exceptional aspirant may request a proficiency evaluation. For the evaluation, the university examines the content expertise and skills of the candidate against the requirements of the program and develops a plan for what the individual must do in terms of coursework, assessments, and other demonstrations of skills to satisfy program and certification requirements. This pathway allows individuals with leadership or administrative experience in a non-education context (e.g., someone with leader training in a military setting) to enter into school leadership (or teaching).

tinuous professional development, and building a collaborative culture. Candidates must present evidence of practice related to the tasks in these areas. These new assessments are expected to drive changes in principal preparation programs. For example, coursework may be reconfigured to better prepare students for success on assessment tasks, and clinical experiences may need to evolve to provide opportunities for students to practice the skills they need to demonstrate through the performance-based assessments (See Box 3.9).

Meanwhile, in Kentucky, revisions to state leadership standards prompted the state to reconsider the rigor and relevance of existing assessments, which led to the decision to drop a previously required assessment (see Box 3.10). This example highlights that policy change need not involve adding or strengthening requirements. Equally important is removing requirements that are not achieving the desired aim.

## Program Approval and Oversight

### How the Program Approval and Oversight Lever Is Used

All UPPI states actively use the program approval lever, but use varies in important ways. In all UPPI states, there is a state entity responsible for program approval and oversight. This responsibility may be housed within an independent or semi-independent professional standards board with regulatory powers (the board performs the approval and

**Box 3.9**
**California Developed a State-Specific Performance Assessment, the CalAPA**

Beginning in 2013, California's professional standards board—the Commission on Teacher Credentialing—required that stage 1 licensure candidates pass a performance-based assessment. The board then led an effort to develop such an assessment. The development effort involved practitioners, administrators, and educators, including representatives from the Association of California School Administrators, the California Association of Professors of Educational Administration, the California Teachers Association, and the California Department of Education. The resultant California Administrator Performance Assessment (CalAPA) requires candidates to demonstrate an ability to investigate, plan, act, and reflect (CTC, 2018). Candidates must provide evidence of leadership practice in the form of video recordings or artifacts. The assessment and scoring rubrics align with the state's program content standards for preparation programs as well as the administrator performance expectations. The assessment is intended to provide both "a formal assessment of candidate administrative ability" and a framework that the administrator preparation program can use to support "candidate preparation and continued professional growth" (CTC, 2019a). The assessment was first administered in fall 2018.

**Box 3.10**
**Kentucky Dropped a Licensure Assessment, Deeming It Poorly Aligned with Current Standards**

The Kentucky Department of Education/Educator Professional Standards Board (KDE/EPSB) assembled a team to review the Kentucky Specialty Test of Instructional and Administrative Practices. The selected-response test concentrates entirely on Kentucky education laws and regulations. The team concluded that the test's focus on laws rather than practical application of leadership standards was not well aligned with current expectations for education leaders in the state. Because state statute mandated that applicants for principal certification complete a specialized assessment on the current instructional and administrative practices in Kentucky public education, the KDE/EPSB could not unilaterally change the requirement. The EPSB identified the removal of this statutory requirements in the Priorities for the 2020 Regular Session of the Kentucky General Assembly. The KDE then worked to identify legislators to sponsor a bill to officially change the statute. During the 2020 Regular Session, the General Assembly passed Senate Bill 174. This bill became effective on July 15, 2020, and amended Kentucky Revised Statute (KRS) 161.027(3) to remove the requirement that applicants for principal certification successfully complete a specialized assessment on the current instructional and administrative practices in Kentucky public education. Thus, the Kentucky Specialty Test is no longer required. Kentucky is retaining its other required assessment, the School Leaders Licensure Assessment (SLLA), because it is aligned with the Professional Standards for Educational Leaders (PSEL). According to interviewees, the SLLA helps the state assess whether principal candidates are learning the required content and can be used to hold preparation programs accountable for their students' performance.

oversight roles). Or responsibility for program approval and oversight may fall to the state board of education or another division within the department of education.

#### *Entities Authorized to Provide Preparation Programs*

State policy determines what types of providers can be authorized to offer state-approved programs that meet licensure requirements. Among UPPI states, most approve not only institutions of higher education, but also districts, county offices, charter organizations, and/or third-party organizations, such as professional associations as providers. Some states authorize different types of organizations for different credentialing pathways. With this approach, they can approve programs that meet specific local needs. For example, in Connecticut, there are two categories of program pathways. The "traditional" program is offered by higher education institutions. The state's alternative program route to certification, in theory, allows for institutions of higher education, local or regional boards of education, regional educational service centers, or nonprofits to offer principal preparation programs that address shortages and support districts that are considered "high need." However, in practice, no such program is currently offered.

States with a two-stage licensure pathway (e.g., each candidate must go through two programs in sequence) have the flexibility to separately approve and oversee programs at the first and/or second stage. In some states, there is a marked difference in the types of institutions providing programs at each stage. Notably, in Florida, 23 out of 25 state-approved stage 1 programs are located in institutions of higher education; the other two programs are housed in school districts. Meanwhile, all of the 66 state-approved stage 2 (principal certification) programs are provided by school districts. In California, 48 out of 66 state-approved traditional stage 1 (provisional credential) programs and 16 out of 53 approved stage 2 (cleared credential) programs are housed in higher education institutions; the remaining programs are provided by a range of organizations, including districts, county offices, and nonprofit organizations. The prevalence of higher education institutions in the first stage and districts in the second stage is important, reflecting greater district involvement in preparation emphasizing on-the-job learning for novice administrators.

#### *Required Program Content and Practices*

Based on a review of the UPPI states' regulations, we found that all seven UPPI states have program approval standards that are distinct from their state leadership standards. These requirements may dictate the content that programs must provide to candidates or the practices they must engage in. Program approval standards or regulations often address the policy areas highlighted by UCEA in Anderson and Reynolds (2015a): partnerships with other institutions and candidates' clinical experiences. In addition, we also found that most UPPI states have regulations relating to the curriculum that programs must offer.

Almost all the UPPI states require principal preparation programs to develop partnerships with other institutions, usually school districts, to meet UCEA's partnership criteria (collaboration on selection, alignment between district and program needs, district agreement to "provide a clinically rich internship"). Sometimes requirements address other criteria, such as collaboration around curriculum development, instructional delivery, evaluation of candidates, completers, and the program itself; mentor and faculty supervisor training; and strategies for continuous improvement.

All UPPI states have state requirements related to clinical experiences that address at least one critical dimension highlighted by Anderson and Reynolds (2015a): deliberately structured, fieldwork integrated with curriculum, core leadership responsibilities, experienced mentors, multiple sites/populations, and 300+ hours of internship. Most UPPI states have regulations that meet at least three of the listed criteria, which is UCEA's benchmark. Few UPPI states meet the requirement that programs provide 300+ hours of field-based experience. Regulations in the UPPI states sometimes include additional requirements around clinical experiences beyond those listed by UCEA. For example, some states have policies specifying the qualifications that supervisors or mentors must meet, the nature of guidance and feedback that candidates must receive, or the manner in which candidates must be evaluated.

With respect to curriculum, many UPPI states have regulations around the content that programs must provide to candidates, but the prescriptiveness varies. Some states focus more on the competencies that candidates must demonstrate by the end of the program, as described in the state's leadership standards, allowing programs latitude in how they support candidates in achieving mastery of those competencies. For example, Florida explicitly states that the "legislative intent is that the focus is on demonstration of competencies, not courses. Specific courses are neither specified nor required by law or rule" (Florida Department of Education, 2017). Other states enumerate the topics and specific content programs must cover. North Carolina regulations require that, beyond addressing the state's leadership standards, programs' coursework address laws and regulations that affect North Carolina public schools, the use of technology, support for struggling students, school climate, evaluation of staff, and other topics. Connecticut similarly requires coursework on specific topics, even outlining the number of hours for one particular course of study. Some states fall somewhere in the middle of the spectrum. For example, California's program standard for curriculum emphasizes the need for coursework and clinical practices to support candidates mastering the state's performance expectations and performance assessment. Requirements around course topics, such as the development of leadership and interpersonal skills or the development of an equity lens, are more implicit throughout the other program standards.

### *State Oversight*

Anderson and Reynolds (2015a) reported that all but one UPPI state meets three or four of UCEA's state oversight criteria ("state review at specified intervals . . . plan for initial oversight . . . [that] includes documentation and/or site visits, [an oversight team with] relevant experience and training . . . and feedback mechanism[s]"). Our review of the current program approval regulations suggests that all UPPI states now require state review at specified intervals, ranging from two to seven years, sometimes with shorter intervals for newly approved programs. California provides one example of what state oversight looks like. The state has a seven-year accreditation cycle that requires programs to collect, analyze, and submit data annually. This accreditation cycle ensures that programs meet common standards of program quality, "which address issues of institutional infrastructure, stability, and processes that are designed to ensure that the implementation of all approved programs is successful" (CTC, 2020b). The accreditation cycle culminates in a site visit from a trained accreditation team and follow-up from the site visit (CTC, 2016).

States have a choice in the extent to which they rely on external accrediting organizations, which could influence the degree of state influence in the approval and oversight process. Reliance on such external accrediting organizations is the norm for institution-wide accreditation in higher education. A few UPPI states depend solely on the accreditation process of the Council for the Accreditation of Educator Preparation (CAEP) (CAEP, 2019c). Most UPPI states use a state-run accreditation process but allow or require programs to pursue CAEP accreditation as well. The CAEP review includes a self-study process, a formative review, and a multi-day site visit conducted by trained reviewers to determine whether programs are meeting its standards (CAEP, 2019a).

### *Program Reporting Requirements*

All UPPI states require preparation programs to report data annually to the state. Examples of required data points include program data (e.g., admission standards, program requirements, and faculty background), student data (e.g., demographics, enrollment), performance data (e.g., completion rates, pass rates for licensure assessments, certification issuance rates), employment data (e.g., placement and rehire rates), and feedback from candidates and employers after program completion. Furthermore, CAEP accreditation requires programs to send CAEP annual reports around similar measures (CTC, 2016). In some states, the regulations also require that these data be published and available to the public. In this respect, the data can be used to support or hold principal preparation programs accountable.

### Examples of Recent Policy Changes Related to Program Approval and Oversight

#### *States adjusted requirements for state-approved preparation programs*

Some UPPI states changed the requirements for state-approved principal preparation programs since 2016. Changes in Kentucky and Florida are expected to result in a greater number of candidates entering preparation programs and therefore a greater number of principals. Kentucky achieved this by removing a requirement for entry into principal preparation programs (see Box 3.11). Meanwhile, Florida approved additional types of institutions offering such programs (see Box 3.12). In contrast, Georgia added program requirements for obtaining principal certification (see Box 3.13).

#### *States shifted the focus of program oversight toward program outcomes*

Policy changes in California, Connecticut, and Florida related to program oversight placed a greater emphasis on the outcomes of program graduates in the program accreditation and approval process in response to concerns that program oversight had been too compliance-driven and focused on process measures. In years prior, program approval standards and processes tended to focus on having programs document how the core curriculum content met the accreditation standards. More recently, the focus has shifted toward the program providing evidence of the quality of the program's candidates and completers, high-quality field experiences, and overall program effectiveness (see Boxes 3.14 and 3.15). These changes were intended to strengthen program quality and, therefore, the potential principal workforce.

#### *Three states launched new systems to better manage the program approval process*

Three states have rolled out systems designed to better manage the program approval process. California, for example, unveiled its Accreditation Data

**Box 3.11**
**Kentucky Removed the Master's Degree as a Requirement for Principal Preparation Program Admission**

As part of a 2018 regulation, Kentucky's Educator Professional Standards Board (EPSB) removed the master's degree as a requirement to enter a principal preparation program. This means that instead of being a post-master's program, principal preparation programs can now terminate in a master's degree. The professional standards board weighed the advantages and disadvantages of teaching experience and educational attainment as prerequisites for entry into an administrative certification program and sought input from institutes of higher education, the state department of education, the commissioner, various administrator associations, and the Council on Postsecondary Education. Some argued that the master's degree requirement helped ensure that candidates had deep content knowledge and experience upon entering the program and promoted the quality of program content. The state department of education and the commissioner, however, were in favor of relaxing the master's requirement. They argued that most other states did not have a master's degree requirement to enter a principal preparation program. Second, they argued that there was little evidence that candidates with a master's degree were more prepared for school leadership or led schools with higher student achievement. Ultimately, the board voted to dissolve the master's degree requirement.

**Box 3.12**
**Florida Approved Additional Institutions to Offer Principal Preparation Programs**

In 2018, Florida's state board of education expanded the types of institutions approved to offer Level I and Level II principal preparation programs (Florida Department of Education, 2018). Under the revised criteria, charter schools, charter management organizations, and school districts became eligible to offer both Level I and Level II programs. Previously, only institutions of higher education could provide Level I programs, and only public school districts could provide Level II programs. The policy change was created in response to concerns around school leader shortages.

**Box 3.13**
**Georgia Approved Principal Preparation Programs Separately for Stage I and Stage II**

As a result of the 2016 change to the two-stage licensure system, Georgia state policymakers revised the requirements for preparation programs. Programs would now be approved separately as preparatory for Stage I or Stage II certification. Aspiring principals needed to complete both programs.

Stage I program approval requirements emphasize coursework but still include a clinical practice component; Stage II program approval requirements involve a 750-hour clinical experience. This staged certification and program structure addressed some perceived limitations rooted in a rule change enacted in 2008.

The 2008 rule (Rule 505-2.58) required educator preparation programs to be performance-based to better prepare candidates to lead on day one. This meant emphasizing clinical experiences. To avoid extending their program length while increasing clinical requirements, some programs began reducing the academic course load. Given fewer courses in which to deliver content, preparation programs increased the prerequisites for program admission. Applicants had to have completed coursework covering leadership skills and concepts. This led to less formal opportunities within a principal preparation program to actually learn the necessary leadership skills.

The 2016 change to a two-stage program, then, essentially expanded the requirements for becoming a principal. School leaders had to complete two programs that together helped ensure that they both received the deep content knowledge and theoretical grounding related to leadership and had opportunities to apply such knowledge and theory in realistic, practical contexts.

System in January 2020 to facilitate the required annual submission of data from program providers. Similarly, preparation programs in Kentucky used to have to submit paper documents directly to the state, but, as of 2018, they can enter their data and responses into an online system managed by the state. Virginia developed its "program credentialing database," an online principal preparation program approval system, using UPPI resources. Launched in 2018, the database replaces the former paper-based system. The provision of this sort of management system may be more of a procedural change than a substantive policy change, but it functions as support for the state mandate to provide the necessary information for program approval or renewal.

#### *States actors encouraged and supported program improvement in a variety of ways*

Several states promoted ongoing program improvement among preparation program providers either by leveraging the state's authority with respect to program renewal or by providing resources and incentives for ongoing program improvement efforts. Florida and Georgia formalized the promotion of ongoing program improvement efforts in rules (see Box 3.16). Although California, Connecticut, and Kentucky did not formalize the idea of self-assessment and continuous improvement in rules, they engaged cohorts of universities and districts in the use of Quality Measures, a principal preparation program self-assessment tool used in UPPI sites. The goal was to push educator preparation

**Box 3.14**
**California Revised Its Accreditation Process to Emphasize Candidate Experience and Performance**

As part of its broad overhaul of policies relating to educational leadership, California's professional standards board—the California Commission on Teacher Credentialing—revised the accreditation process to privilege data related to the experiences and performance of candidates. These data are gathered, for example, through surveys of candidates, employers, supervising faculty of clinical practice, and, most notably, the California Administrator Performance Assessment (CalAPA). As noted earlier, the commission intends to use data from the assessment to bolster and inform its accreditation process and support program continuous improvement.

**Box 3.15**
**Connecticut Will Begin Using Program Outcome Data for Continued Program Approval**

As required by existing statute, Connecticut will build and begin using program outcome data in an Educator Preparation Program Data Dashboard in conjunction with accreditation findings to inform continuing program approval for leadership preparation programs. A similar dashboard for teacher preparation has already been implemented. Accountability indicators in the dashboard will include program enrollment and completer rates, pass rates for licensure exams, employment data, feedback survey data from candidates and employers, certification issuance rates, and diversity data. Educator preparation programs must report dashboard data annually for each preparation program. If the annual data suggest that there may be concerns about program quality, the Connecticut State Department of Education can conduct an interim visit in the middle of the seven-year accreditation cycle.

**Box 3.16**
**Florida and Georgia Formalized the Promotion of Ongoing Program Improvement Efforts in Rules**

In Florida, Statute 1012.562 and State Board of Education Rule 6A-5.081 operationalized changes to the state's program approval process. Effective December 2016, stage 1 programs were required to work with district partners to determine program admission standards, identify and select candidates, provide job-embedded field experiences for candidates, and identify strategies for continuous improvement.

In Georgia, a rule effective July 2018 recommended that program providers in Georgia conduct a formative self-assessment around the midpoint of their seven-year program approval cycle. One interviewee shared that the state stopped short of mandating this process, not wanting to be regarded as imposing requirements upon providers. The state did, however, acclimate providers to this idea by leading cohorts of providers through the use of Quality Measures.

**Box 3.17**
**Connecticut Encouraged Continuous Program Improvement with Incentives**

Connecticut's state department of education activated the incentives mechanism in encouraging continuous program improvement. It offered a modest grant to principal preparation program providers that entered into a two-year agreement with the department of education. The programs were to identify their areas of strength and areas for improvement based on the Quality Measures exercise. Then, they had to create a short-term plan that would fit into a longer-term program improvement plan.

programs to think about best practices as they relate to leadership programs (see Box 3.17).

All UPPI states stimulate improvements in program quality by sponsoring statewide convenings to disseminate best or innovative practices in principal preparation, including work related to program redesign at UPPI sites. The California Commission on Teacher Credentialing held a series of meetings for program providers around the implementation of the California Administrator Performance Assessment, at which universities undertaking program redesign in response to the new assessment—particularly UPPI grantee San Diego State University—shared insights from their process. In Florida, the Florida Association of Professors of Educational Leadership held a session focused on levers to strengthen stage 1 educational leadership programs, with a specific focus on fortifying partnerships between districts and program providers. Meanwhile, Georgia introduced leadership programming into its long-standing annual conferences with program providers. Conference sessions included the use of Quality Measures, relevance of leader dispositions, and challenges that programs face. Many states indicated that they had not had convenings focused explicitly on principal preparation prior to UPPI.

## Professional Development

### How the Professional Development Lever Is Used

UPPI states utilize the professional development lever in three notable ways: connecting it with licensure, providing resources or direct assistance, and establishing requirements for districts around providing professional development.

Most UPPI states utilize licensure and licensure renewal to promote principal professional development. They do so by requiring novice administrators to participate in professional development or requiring credentialed administrators to participate in professional development to renew their licenses. For example, licensure renewal instructions in Virginia require principals to complete 270 "professional development points" (Virginia Department of Education, 2019a). Points are assigned based on the type of professional development, such as one semester hour of college credit equals 30 points. Georgia requires principals to engage in continual professional development via their local unit administration professional learning community (Georgia Professional Standards Commission, 2020).

All UPPI states support professional development through guidance, resources, or technical assistance. Virginia provides a list of district contacts via its Professional Learning Network platform. The platform supports districts learning from one another about promising practices in a range of areas, including principal professional development (Virginia Department of Education, 2020). In Georgia, the professional standards board hosts an annual conference for certification and program officials with sessions focused on leadership. In 2018, the UPPI grant supported the Elevating Educational Leadership Conference in Georgia, focused on professional learning for school leaders. In addition, the Georgia Department of Education and the Governor's Office of Student Achievement provide principal professional development directly. Several other states provide resources, such as a calendar of events or list of state professional development opportunities.

All UPPI states also have administrator or principal associations that support new and seasoned principals through conferences, programs, resources, and mentorship. For example, the Georgia Educational Leadership Faculty Association conducts an annual conference for education leaders to share lessons learned and innovative techniques. The North Carolina Principals and Assistant Principals Association offers professional development for principals and assistant principals through the Distinguished Leadership in Practice program and Future-Ready Leadership program, respectively.

Most UPPI states have established standards or requirements for districts regarding providing professional development. Florida prescribes the elements that districts must include in their professional development systems, stating that the system "must align to the standards adopted by the state (in the Evaluation Protocol incorporated into SBE rule 6A-5.071) and support the framework for standards adopted by the National Staff Development Council" (Florida Legislature, 2019). The Florida Department of Education does not approve or recommend professional development programs or courses to districts, but it does provide links to professional learning resources (Florida Department of Education, 2020). Likewise, Kentucky influences the professional development activities within districts by requiring them to design professional development plans (Kentucky Legislature, 2020) that include six elements outlined in the regulation, such as objectives focused on the school and district mission.

### Examples of Recent Policy Changes Related to Professional Development

#### *States created or expanded opportunities to support principal professional development*

Several states undertook new efforts to support principal professional development by establishing new programs or increasing funding for existing programs. The two UPPI states (California and North Carolina) that took the 3-percent ESSA set-aside committed to leveraging those funds to support the growth and development of principals and school leaders. In North Carolina, the state had already been operating the Principal READY program; it rolled out the companion Assistant Principal READY program with the ESSA funding. These two programs, aligned with state leadership standards, included statewide learning sessions for sitting school leaders designed to address the skills they need to provide high-quality feedback to teachers.

Beyond the ESSA set-aside, California made other financial investments in principal professional development. The state's 2019–2020 budget allocated $13.8 million in ongoing federal funds to form the 21st Century California Leadership Academy. The competitive grant program solicited proposals from professional development providers, including districts, institutes of higher education, and nonprofit organizations, to compete for grants and opportunities to provide professional learning to K–12 school leaders in alignment with the statewide system of support. The purpose of the grants is to ensure that districts across the state eligible for Title II funds would have free access to high-quality professional development opportunities for their administrators. Meanwhile, Virginia used Title II funds to expand its School-University Research Network Principal Academy (see Box 3.18).

In other cases, as exemplified by Georgia's Governor's School Leadership Academy (Box 3.19) and the Kentucky Department of Education (Box 3.20), the state directly provides principal professional development.

Finally, the Connecticut State Department of Education has also leveraged the information mechanism. Drawing on UPPI funding, it created a comprehensive resource guide designed to support new administrators. The guide covers critical topics that a school leader in Connecticut should know, from school safety and security to types and purposes of assessments, to educational law. The department regards this as a first step in an extended plan to provide a statewide universal support mechanism for early career educators. State leaders decided that disseminating resources to principals, aspirants, districts, and preparation programs can be more effective and expedient at

**Box 3.18**
**Virginia Invested in the School-University Research Network Principal Academy**

The School-University Research Network in Virginia is a long-standing partnership between the School of Education at the College of William and Mary and more than 30 districts throughout the state. The Principal Academy was an existing initiative designed to improve principals' (and assistant principals') instructional knowledge and to develop mentor principals who would support future cohorts of leaders. In this two-year-long program, participants—about 40 in a cohort—engage in a range of activities with each other and with mentors. These activities include co-observing instruction with an observation tool, planning and developing professional development for teachers, and conducting an action research project. The academy had been funded by grants external to the state department of education. In 2018, the Virginia Department of Education committed two years of funding toward the program. The contribution consisted mostly of Title II funds, supplemented by UPPI resources in one year.

**Box 3.19**
**Georgia's Governor's School Leadership Academy Provides Support for Principals in Low-Performing Schools**

In May 2018, the Georgia governor instituted the Governor's School Leadership Academy through the Governor's Office of Student Achievement. As one of four professional development programs offered by the academy, the Principal Support Program serves principals in chronically low-performing schools by providing cohort-based learning and networking opportunities, one-on-one coaching and mentorship, and support and feedback for job-embedded tasks and competencies. The Principal Support Program was designed to further develop principals already on the job in federally designated schools (i.e., Comprehensive Support and Improvement [CSI], Targeted Support and Improvement [TSI], Promise, or School Improvement Grant [SIG] schools) (Georgia Governor's Office of Student Achievement, 2020b). Through an ongoing partnership with the Georgia Department of Education School Improvement Division, goals and outcomes for the program are aligned with state requirements, School Effectiveness and District Effectiveness Specialists attend cohort sessions with the principals they support, and support activities are coordinated between the state agencies.

changing practice than making policy and statute changes can.

**Box 3.20**
**Kentucky Will Provide Coaching Training to Sitting Principals and Those Who Develop Principals**

In collaboration with regional cooperatives, the Kentucky Department of Education (KDE) plans to provide training on coaching models to principals in the Principal Partnership Project (P3) program in late 2020. Established in 2015, P3 offers free individualized support to newer principals in Kentucky through training and networking opportunities. In addition, to help establish continuity between principal preparation and practice, the KDE will provide funding for each principal preparation program to send a faculty member to receive the training. The faculty members commit to making a plan for disseminating, implementing, and sustaining the coaching approach within their programs. KDE's vision is to position coaching as a shared, statewide practice for supporting school leaders and a practice that leaders themselves can use to be effective in their role. That is, preparation programs can train university-based clinical experience supervisors to use coaching to help principal candidates improve their skills. Meanwhile, some principals in the field are learning to use coaching to support their teachers. Many of these principals may, in turn, mentor principal candidates who will be familiar with the coaching approach.

## Evaluation

### How the Evaluation Lever Is Used

We identified five common principal evaluation system requirements: use of student growth data in evaluation, annual evaluations for all principals, use of survey data in evaluation, use of observations in evaluation, and use of plans to support struggling principals (National Center for Teacher Quality, 2019). A few UPPI states had requirements in all five areas, while a few states had none of the requirements. Below, we present some examples of ways states influence the quality of school leadership across the state.

One way states influence principal quality through the evaluation lever is by requiring districts to use frameworks in evaluating principals. A clear and concise structure, such as Georgia's Leader Keys Effectiveness System (LKES), presents districts with multiple measures that are aligned to evidence-based standards, indicators for measuring principal performance and effectiveness, metrics based on state assessments (e.g., student growth), and a data system that is managed and monitored by the state. Other states build explicit requirements into a flexible evaluation structure without an explicit framework or indicators. Florida, for example, requires that at least one-third of the evaluation be based on student performance, although districts may choose to utilize higher percentages. Another approach is for states to provide guidance and resources for districts to use when designing their own evaluations. For example, California's evaluations can be based on the California Professional Standards for Education Leaders, and the evaluation should include measures of student academic growth, among other items.

States can also regulate district evaluation processes. For example, Georgia requires districts to "adhere to processes, guidelines, and procedures" outlined in the LKES (Georgia Department of Education, 2016). Some states require districts to submit their evaluation plans for review by the state while granting them the freedom to develop the system to meet their unique needs and environment.

Finally, states can monitor statewide principal quality or encourage districts to do so by setting data system reporting requirements for principal evaluation. Currently, none of the UPPI states requires districts to report principal evaluation data to the state, but some provide guidance on how the district should set up their own data system, particularly one aligned with the state's evaluation guidelines. One UPPI state requires districts to have their data systems reviewed and approved by the state.

### Examples of Recent Policy Changes Related to Evaluation

#### *States aligned leader evaluation with state/national leadership standards*

Following the adoption of state/national leadership standards, Kentucky and Georgia moved toward aligning principal evaluation criteria to the new standards. In Georgia, Albany State University led the effort to align the Leader Assessment on Performance Standards (the component of the state's principal evaluation system that covers leader practices) to the state standards for school leaders. The university initiated an effort to cross-walk the two sets of standards. That activity revealed gaps in the evaluation standards, particularly with concerns with equity and cultural responsiveness. In Kentucky, the department of education led the charge to align the evaluation standards to the PSEL (see Box 3.21). These activities aimed to directly change district evaluation practices and indirectly influence program providers as they strive to prepare candidates to succeed in a district leadership role. Sitting principals are also indirect targets of influence for such mandates, as the new evaluation standards could provide incentives that shift their behavior.

> **Box 3.21**
> **Kentucky Aligned Evaluation Standards to PSEL to Create Continuity Between Preparation and Service Box**
>
> In 2019, after adopting the Professional Standards for Educational Leaders (PSEL) as the state leader standards, the Kentucky Department of Education (KDE) amended the Kentucky Framework for Personnel Evaluation so the evaluation standards for principals and assistant principals align to PSEL as well. The impetus was to have all entities from pre-kindergarten through postsecondary using the same standards for principals—from preparation to evaluation. The amendment was expected to be effective in summer 2020 and be a state requirement beginning fall 2020.
>
> To support districts' transition to these new principal evaluation standards, KDE has developed a guidance document that works through what each standard means. In addition, KDE will provide online modules to help principal evaluators and supervisors implement the standards in practice.

#### *States weighed importance of student growth scores in leader evaluation*

Three UPPI states enacted policy changes to principal evaluation that altered the way in which the evaluation system accounts for student growth scores or tied some compensation to student growth. In Georgia, a 2016 law reduced the weight of student test scores for school leader (and teacher) evaluations, from 70 percent to 40 percent. The intent of the policy change was to allow teachers and leaders to focus their attention more on classroom and school practices. Also in 2016, the Connecticut State Board adopted the Performance Evaluation Advisory Council's recommendation that student state assessment data not be used to determine educators' (teachers' and school administrators') rating in the evaluation system. Such data should continue to inform goal setting and professional development for school improvement. Meanwhile, North Carolina has a state salary schedule for principals (and other public-school personnel), which means that state policy influences principal compensation (North Carolina Department of Public Instruction, 2019). The state's 2017 appropriations act (SB 257) led to an increase in the average base pay of principals and changed the determinants of principal compensation (BEST NC, 2017). This included a new performance pay component based on students' standardized test scores (see Box 3.22).

**Box 3.22**
**North Carolina's New System for Determining Principal Compensation Included a Component Based on Student Growth**

Prior to 2017, principal pay in North Carolina was tied to advanced degree attainment, years of experience, number of teachers in the school, and longevity in the position. In 2017, a system of determining principal compensation was introduced wherein principal pay was tied to the number of students enrolled in the school. This system also included a performance pay component, giving principals an opportunity to earn bonuses based on the magnitude of growth in student standardized test scores in the school. While these 2017 changes aimed to reward principals working in turnaround schools, professional educator groups and media reports expressed concern about whether the approach for calculating bonuses would achieve that aim. In addition, observers were concerned that experienced principals with advanced degrees would be subject to pay cuts and leave the system. As a result, Governor Roy Cooper's proposed 2019–2021 budget included an experience-based salary schedule for principals that addressed stakeholder concerns. SB 170, introduced in March 2019, provided bonuses to more principals. All principals who supervised a school in the top 50th percentile of school growth the previous year would receive a bonus.

## Leader Tracking Systems

### How the Leader Tracking Lever Is Used

As of 2019, none of the UPPI states had a state-level data system linking principal preparation programs to a range of outcomes for program participants. Some states could link programs to licensure. North Carolina, for example, has a robust state data system covering educators and school and student outcomes, and an interactive dashboard providing information linking teacher preparation programs to performance outcomes (University of North Carolina System, 2020). As part of UPPI, North Carolina was working toward the launch of a leadership dashboard in the 2019–2020 school year. Meanwhile,

Florida was also considering how the state might incentivize and support "the development of district- or consortia-based database management systems that collect and aggregate data on leader preparation, leadership development, and leadership performance outcomes to support placement, planning, and decision-making at the school district level" (School Educational Leadership Enhancement Committee Task Force [SELECT], 2018, p. 5). Until recently then, leader tracking has been largely unexplored as a lever for improving principal quality statewide.

**Examples of Recent Policy Changes Related to Leader Tracking Systems**

***One state will build statewide leader tracking systems; in others states, leader tracking systems play a supporting role in tracking leader development***

North Carolina is aiming to build a statewide data system focused on school leaders—a leader tracking system. Through an effort spearheaded by the state superintendent, the department of public instruction has been developing a Leadership Data Dashboard (LDD), which was slated to launch late in the 2019–2020 school year (see Box 3.23).

Other states are playing a facilitative role by fostering statewide conversations about the need for and the use of data systems to promote principal quality or supporting efforts centered in preparation programs. In Kentucky, programs recognized a need to better track candidate progress and elicit feedback from candidates after they leave the program. Among other things, the state's move to adopt CAEP standards for state program accreditation requires programs to draw on robust data related to graduate outcomes in order to provide evidence of program effectiveness. EPSB/KDE had planned a meeting in

**Box 3.23**
**North Carolina Is Building a Leader Data Dashboard**

North Carolina contracted with SAS Institute to build the Leader Data Dashboard (LDD). SAS Institute provides data services and analysis for the North Carolina Department of Public Instruction (NC DPI) on other topics. System development involved thinking through how data would be shared among and accessed by the NC DPI, University of North Carolina General Administration (UNC-GA), universities, districts, and SAS Institute. As of spring 2018, the NC DPI envisioned establishing a data sharing agreement with the UNC-GA, which would then share aggregated data (e.g., principal evaluation data) as needed with its constituent universities for program improvement purposes. Meanwhile, districts would have access to individual principal-level data for principals in their district and aggregate data from other districts through another SAS platform. Districts could use the system to support data-driven decisionmaking and succession planning within their own district and to compare or benchmark their district's performance against that of other districts.

A statewide leader tracking system was attractive and feasible in North Carolina in part because the NC DPI, with support from SAS Institute, already had a comprehensive statewide data system in place covering K–12 and higher education that could serve as a starting point for the new system. NC DPI viewed a statewide system as more desirable than a system owned by or only accessible to a few UPPI districts. A statewide system would entail minimal costs beyond a district-level system, yet would benefit districts across the state.

spring 2020 for principal preparation programs to visit and learn from Western Kentucky University, the state's UPPI site, which has been developing a leader tracking system within the university. Other providers may be able to contract with Western Kentucky University to use its tracking system or build out their own.

## Summary of Lever Use and Policy Change

In Table 3.2, we summarize the prevalence of use of key policy lever activities as described in this chapter. This summary highlights that the prevalence of lever use varies and some activities are more common than others. The table suggests that standards, licensure, program approval and oversight, and professional development are core levers in which key activities are performed by all or most states.

Table 3.3 summarizes the types of policy changes we observed by lever as described in this chapter. Most activities were undertaken by only a few states. The adoption of new licensure assessments and new efforts to support principal professional development were the most common areas of policy change.

**Table 3.2**
**Prevalence of Key Policy Actions, by Policy Lever**

| Policy Lever | Key Policy Actions | Prevalence of Use Among UPPI States |
|---|---|---|
| Standards | • Adopt state standards for school principals<br>• Promote the use of state standards | • All<br>• All |
| Recruitment of aspiring leaders | • Establish prerequisites for program participation<br>• Subsidize participation in pre-service programs<br>• Encourage effective program recruitment practice | • All<br>• Few<br>• Most |
| Licensure | • Determine licensure pathways<br>• Determine licensure requirements | • All<br>• All |
| Program approval and oversight | • Determine types of providers that can offer programs<br>• Establish criteria for program approval/renewal<br>• Approve programs<br>• Specify program content/structure | • All<br>• All<br>• All<br>• Most |
| Professional development | • Establish requirements for principal professional development<br>• Support or offer principal professional development | • Most<br>• All |
| Evaluation | • Establish content criteria<br>• Establish process expectations<br>• Establish reporting requirements | • Few<br>• Few<br>• Few |
| Leader tracking systems | • Support data systems for tracking aspiring and current principals | • None |

NOTE: Few = 1–3 of the states; most = 4–6 of the states.

**Table 3.3**
**Policy Changes, by Policy Lever**

| Policy Lever | Policy Change | Prevalence of Such Change Among UPPI States |
|---|---|---|
| Standards | • Update state standards for school principals | • Few |
| Recruitment of aspiring leaders | • Subsidize participation in pre-service programs | • Few |
| Licensure | • Revise licensure pathways<br>• Adopt new licensure assessments | • Few<br>• Most |
| Program approval and oversight | • Change program requirements<br>• Shift focus of program oversight toward outcomes<br>• Improve procedural aspects of program approval<br>• Encourage or support program improvement | • Few<br>• Few<br>• Few<br>• Few |
| Professional development | • Expand efforts to support principal professional development | • Most |
| Evaluation | • Align evaluation with state standards<br>• Reduce emphasis of student achievement growth in evaluation<br>• Introduce performance pay for principals based on achievement | • Few<br>• Few<br>• Few |
| Leader tracking systems | • Provide support for the development of a statewide data system for tracking aspiring and current principals | • Few |

NOTE: Few = 1–3 of the states; most = 4–6 of the states.

## How Levers Exert Influence on Principal Quality

Our review of the use of policy levers in UPPI states suggests that the levers can be mapped onto the pathway to the principalship to highlight opportunities for using the lever (see Figure 3.1). Based on evidence from the UPPI states, we hypothesize that the recruitment, professional development, and evaluation levers tend to operate at the beginning or end of the pathway. Program approval and oversight and licensure levers operate at various points of the pathway, and the two-stage pathway provides additional opportunities for state action. Standards and leader tracking systems operate (or have the potential to operate) across the entire pathway.

Policy levers serve as "mechanisms that translate . . . policy goals . . . into concrete actions" (McDonnell and Elmore, 1987, p. 134). There is a vast body of research on policy levers that seeks to enhance understanding about their intended impact and the reasons why one instrument or set of instruments is used rather than others. This literature, which spans policy areas, categorizes policy instruments in a variety of ways. The literature consistently identifies a "spectrum of influence" for policy levers; levers can (1) require actions through **mandates**, authority, or rules, (2) encourage actions

**Figure 3.1**
**Policy Levers Mapped onto the Generalized Program Pathway to the Principalship**

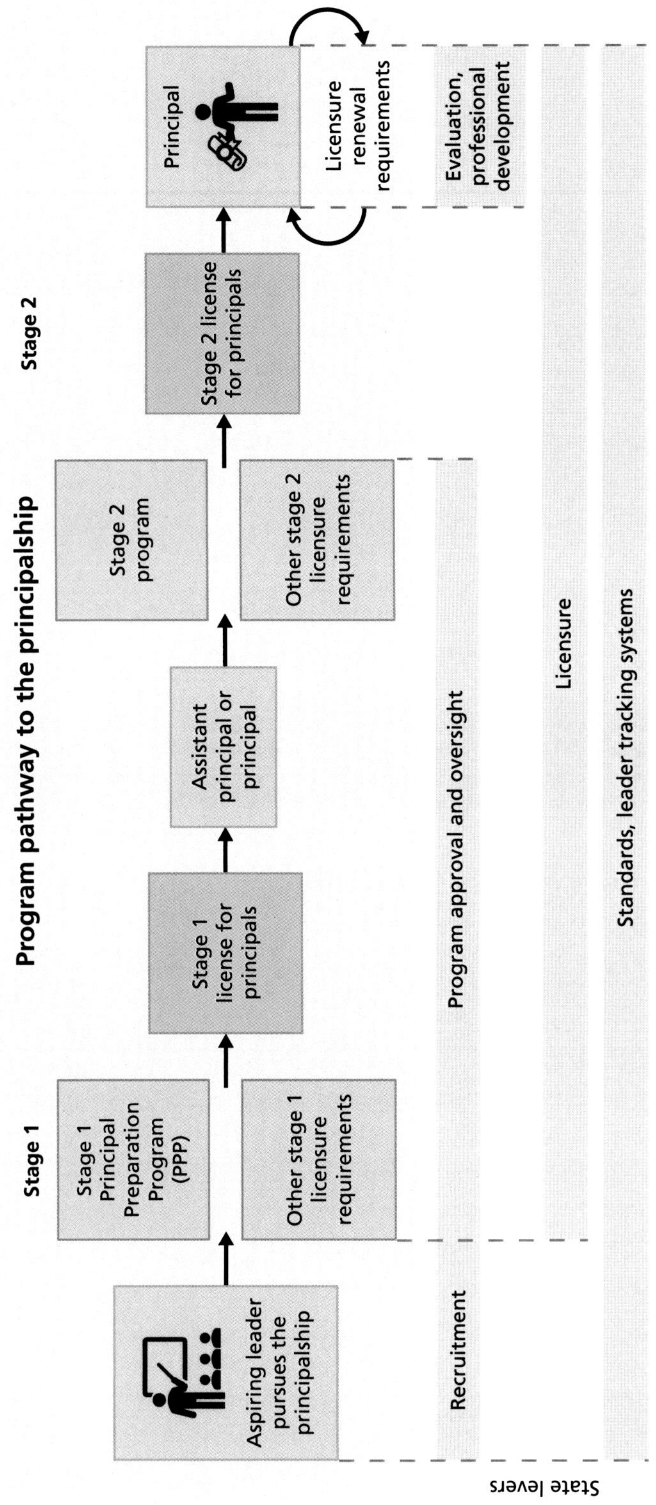

through the use of **incentives** or inducements, such as financial resources, (3) and build capacity for action through **information-sharing**, guidance, or collaboration (Shroff et al., 2012; Capano and Hewlett, 2020). These actions are ways in which the policy levers aim to shape the actions or perspectives of stakeholders or "policy targets" (Capano and Hewlett, 2020).

In some cases, the policy instruments encourage the policy target to follow a particular process. For example, a requirement that principal preparation programs partner with districts would be a procedural mandate. In other cases, the policy lever promotes particular values, standards, or perspectives. One example would be a requirement that aspiring principals pass a specific licensure examination, which sets an overall quality benchmark or standard. In our review of the use of policy levers in the seven UPPI states, we observed examples of policy instruments driving both processes and standards. We also observed all three categories of policy instruments: mandates, incentives, and information-sharing.

Drawing on observations from the UPPI states, we associate each lever with a primary spectrum of influence category through which the lever operates (see Table 3.4). Though we did not list them, in some cases, there are multiple spectrum of influence categories, and the spectrum of influence does not operate the same way in every state (e.g., evaluation is not a mandate in every state). We also provide an example to illustrate the use of the policy lever via that primary mechanism.

Three key state policy levers for enhancing the quality of principals operate as mandates: licensure, program approval and oversight, and evaluation. Leader tracking systems could potentially operate as a mandate or incentive, depending on whether the state required programs and districts to submit data into the system and make use of the system. However, we did not observe any of the UPPI states using that lever at the state level as yet.

Policy levers strive to influence behavior (Capano and Hewlett, 2020). In examining state policy levers that seek to improve principal quality, we observed examples of instruments targeting the behavior and actions of aspiring and current principals, preparation programs, districts, and professional development providers.

In Table 3.5, we summarize the primary (highlighted in yellow) and secondary policy targets (shaded in gray) of each lever. The primary policy target is the stakeholder or stakeholders whose behavior must be influenced directly in order for the policy lever to be effective. The secondary policy targets are stakeholders whose behavior could be influenced either directly or indirectly.

Several key insights arise from looking at the array of likely stakeholders affected (policy targets) by policy levers. The first is that levers typically each have primary targets, although there may be nuances depending on state-specific policies. Regardless, most levers have secondary impacts on the behaviors of other stakeholder groups, highlighting the importance of understanding the ripple effects of change for any

**Table 3.4**
**Spectrum of Influence for Policy Levers**

| Policy Lever | Spectrum of Influence | Example |
|---|---|---|
| Standards | Information-sharing | State develops rubric to help preparation programs align courses with standards |
| Recruitment of aspiring leaders | Incentive | State-supported program that identifies and supports aspiring leaders |
| Licensure | Mandate | Licensure requirements for induction and renewal |
| Program approval and oversight | Mandate | Approval and reporting requirements |
| Professional development | Information-sharing | State-supported resources and catalogs of professional development offerings |
| Evaluation | Mandate | State requires districts to apply specific evaluation criteria and processes |
| Leader tracking systems | Not applicable | Not applicable |

**Table 3.5**
**Policy Targets for Policy Levers**

| | Stakeholders Affected | | | | |
|---|---|---|---|---|---|
| Policy Lever | Preparation Programs | Districts | Current Principals | Aspiring Principals | Professional Development Providers |
| Standards | X | X | X | X | N/A |
| Recruitment of aspiring leaders | X | X | N/A | X | N/A |
| Licensure | X | X | X | X | N/A |
| Program approval and oversight | X | X | N/A | X | N/A |
| Professional development | N/A | X | X | N/A | X |
| Evaluation | N/A | X | X | N/A | N/A |
| Leader tracking systems | N/A | N/A | N/A | N/A | N/A |

NOTE: Yellow shading indicates primary policy targets, and gray shading indicates secondary policy targets.

given lever, and also the ability of state policy to achieve similar goals of, for example, improving preparation program quality through different means or levers.

Of the three levers for which the primary influence mechanism was mandates (licensure, program approval and oversight, and evaluation), the two used by all states (licensure and program approval and oversight) have aspiring principals, current principals, or preparation programs, but not districts, as primary policy targets. Additionally, we noted that states were generally less inclined to impose direct mandates on districts in comparison with aspiring principals, current principals, and preparation programs, perhaps in deference to local control.

Having described the use of policy levers and examples of policy change, we turn in the next chapter to a discussion about the cross-cutting themes related to policy lever use.

CHAPTER FOUR

# Perspectives on the Effective Use of Policy Levers

In this chapter, we address our third research question by focusing on what we have learned across UPPI sites about the effective use of the seven policy levers. These themes emerged from our interviews with state stakeholders. More details about the stakeholders we interviewed and the questions we asked them are available in Appendix A. We begin with a discussion of how stakeholders, in the aggregate, view the use of each lever. Next, we call out examples of interconnectedness—across levers and across targets of influence within levers—highlighting ways in which interconnectedness can help extend the use of levers. Finally, we describe common factors that appear to influence the effectiveness of the levers.

## Stakeholder Views on the Effectiveness of the Levers

During interviews, we asked key state stakeholders to report their level of agreement or disagreement with a statement about the degree to which the state is using a particular lever effectively to promote principal quality. We then probed the reasons for that assessment. Stakeholder views about the effectiveness of state-level efforts varied by lever, across and within states, and by stakeholder group.

### States appear to emphasize different levers

Table 4.1 provides a broad overview of responses by lever and by state. Looking down the columns, stakeholder responses suggest that states emphasize different constellations of levers to promote principal quality. In no state did a majority of stakeholders report that the state was using all levers effectively. The highest number of levers for which there was agreement was five (Virginia).

### Across states, interviewees agreed that the standards and program approval levers are used effectively

Looking across the rows in Table 4.1, we see that the standards lever was the only lever for which a majority of stakeholders in all states agreed that the lever was being used effectively. A majority of stakeholders also expressed approval for the way the program

**Table 4.1**
**Majority (50% or More) of Stakeholders Agreed That Use of Lever in State Is Effective, by Lever and by State**

| Policy Lever | California | Connecticut | Florida | Georgia | Kentucky | North Carolina | Virginia |
|---|---|---|---|---|---|---|---|
| Standards | X | X | X | X | X | X | X |
| Recruitment of aspiring leaders | | | | | | X | |
| Licensure | X | | X | X | | | X |
| Program approval and oversight | X | X | | X | X | | X |
| Professional development | | X | X | | | | X |
| Evaluation | | | X | | | | X |
| Leader tracking systems | | | | | | | |

NOTE: Responses were analyzed as Agree, Disagree, Neutral, or No response; lack of a mark indicating majority agreement should therefore not be interpreted as disagreement.

approval lever was being used, with most interviewees in five states agreeing that the lever was being used effectively.

There was less agreement about the use of other levers. In four states, a majority of interviewees agreed that the licensure lever was being used effectively. In three states, a majority of stakeholders agreed that the professional development lever was being used effectively. Interviewees suggested that state-level involvement in professional development was minimal, with districts or individuals bearing primary responsibility for identifying and providing professional development; there is a lack of support from the state to fund the efforts or even direct the attention of districts to worthy options. In the few states for which stakeholders indicated that their state's efforts were effective, there was funding allocated for professional development and state-supported programs.

### Across states, most interviewee groups indicated that the leader tracking, evaluation, and recruitment levers were not used effectively

In only two states did a majority of stakeholders agree that the evaluation lever was being used effectively to promote principal quality. In only one state did a majority of stakeholders agree that the recruitment lever was used effectively. And in no state did a majority of stakeholders report that statewide leader tracking systems were used effectively to promote principal quality.

These perspectives could indicate either that the state was not using the lever at all or that the state was using the lever but not doing so effectively. With regard to leader tracking and evaluation, the former appears to be the case. With regard to recruitment, our review suggests that the recruitment and selection lever is being used by most UPPI states—most commonly in conjunction with the program approval or licensure lever—but interview responses suggested that stakeholders did not consider that use to be effective. Interviewees explained that their state did not effectively promote recruitment into pre-service preparation, either because recruitment was not widely recognized as influencing principal quality or because the state's recruitment policies were not effective. Only interviewees in North Carolina—which has a long-standing statewide program to support aspiring leaders—consistently agreed that the state effectively uses this lever to improve the quality of school leadership in the state. In addition, one stakeholder explained that recruitment was not widely recognized as influencing principal quality, explaining that "there has been no signal, guidance, or policy from the state department." Interviewees noted that people self-select into the leadership path and that districts rather than the state are involved in recruitment. Several districts or conglomerations of districts have committed to "growing their own leaders" and may provide financial incentives to support promising candidates in pursuing a principal preparation program. In a similar fashion, stakeholders reported that evaluation is an area where districts have responsibility and a large amount of autonomy and where state guidance and support are limited.

#### Across roles, there was convergence about states' use of three levers

We also analyzed stakeholder responses within each state by role. Specifically, we identified each respondent as a representative from one of these six organizations (see Appendix A for more details on this analysis):

- state government, including legislators and representatives from the governor's office
- state departments of education or professional standards boards, including the commissioner or state superintendent of education, state board of education representatives, and UPPI state partner leads
- educational cooperatives or county offices
- districts or related associations, including state associations of school administrators
- university faculty, including UPPI university-based leads, faculty association representatives, and university administrators, including deans and provosts
- nonprofit or advocacy organizations.

The majority of these six role groups in each state converged on their assessment of state efforts in the use of standards, recruitment, and leader tracking.

The standards lever was felt to be used effectively across role groups in most states. In five states, all roles represented among interviewed stakeholders unanimously agreed that it was effectively used as a policy lever in the state. The state government in the sixth state had a dissenting view. In the seventh state, the state department of education or professional educator standards board and those in a university-based role held a favorable view of the state's use of standards, while districts disagreed; other roles registered neutral responses.

Role groups in a majority of states indicated that leader tracking was not being used effectively. In five states, all role groups that presented an opinion about leader tracking unanimously disagreed that it was effectively used as a policy lever in the state. The state government in the sixth state and a nonprofit in the seventh state had more-favorable views. Recruitment was also felt not to be used effectively by role groups in a majority of states. In four states, role groups unanimously disagreed that recruitment was effectively used. In two other states, the state department of education or professional educator standards board held the lone favorable view of state efforts in recruitment. As mentioned previously, North Carolina is the positive outlier, with all role groups agreeing that state efforts in recruitment have been effective.

#### Respondents in different roles perceived states' use of other levers differently, usually in relation to their sphere of control

Across roles, there were some differences in perceptions of the effectiveness of other levers. Broadly, where there were notable differences, the role groups that considered a lever to be used effectively had primary responsibility for the lever (i.e., it was within their sphere of control). On the other hand, those that disagreed about a lever's effectiveness were not primarily responsible for that lever. For example, in all five states in which there was not a unanimous agreement about the effective use of licensure, the state department of education or professional educator standards board and university stakeholders held the more favorable view. These two sets of actors have the most direct role in setting policies or taking actions to influence candidates' path to licensure directly. Meanwhile, in all five states, district representatives, who arguably have little role in licensure, disagreed. For all other role groups, there was no clear pattern. Similarly, in the states in which there was not agreement about the use of program approval and oversight, all the departments of education or professional educator standards boards agreed that this lever was used effectively; however, districts that traditionally have had little voice in university programming disagreed.

#### Role groups involved earlier on the principal pathway tended to view state use of levers as effective

Differences in perspectives may also be attributable to a role group's involvement on the pathway to the principalship. Broadly, those role groups working closely with principals earlier on the pathway or dealing with program-related levers and issues (i.e., state departments of education and universities) tended more often to endorse a lever's effectiveness. As can be inferred in the examples provided above, departments of education or professional educator standards boards and university roles tended to view the levers as effective. In most states, respondents in these roles viewed all levers except recruitment and leader tracking as effective. These optimistic assessments of the state's use of levers to promote principal quality likely occur because those involved in earlier pathway activities rarely receive direct feedback about principal quality in the field. On the other hand, those working with principals in roles on the ground—namely, districts—were more critical of the effectiveness of the levers. Indeed, districts in most states agreed only that the standards lever is being used effectively. Districts' view of the effectiveness of various levers to improve principal quality is likely informed by the potential hires or principals they encounter daily.

The one lever that does not fit the pattern just described is evaluation. In states lacking agreement about the use of this lever, most districts, which primarily bear responsibility for and have autonomy in the evaluation process, did not view it as effective. Meanwhile, state departments of education or professional educator standards boards and universities agreed that it was effective. This makes sense insofar as districts, as the end consumer or employer of principals, have the most direct insight into whether principals are effective. Altogether, our analyses by role suggest that more research to understand the differing perspectives of states' use of policy levers.

Lastly, views around the professional development lever tended to be unsettled across role groups, and in no state was there a consensus among roles around how effectively this lever was used. Across the seven states, nonprofit organizations concurred that this lever was not effective. While more state departments of education or professional educator standards boards viewed the professional development lever favorably, and more districts viewed the lever as ineffective, the pattern is nuanced. That is, in three states, the department of education or professional educator standards board held a more favorable view, but in three other states, the two groups landed on the same side (i.e., both essentially agreed or disagreed). Similarly, while universities tended to side with the departments of education or professional educator standards board, this was not always the case. No patterns emerged among other roles with respect to the effective use of evaluation.

## Interconnectedness Across Levers

We found that the state policy levers are highly interconnected. This is important because the challenge facing policymakers is to identify not the single best policy lever, but rather the optimal policy mix of levers. Given constraints and preferences, policy levers can have more powerful effects when used in complementary and connected ways (Howlett, 2017; Shroff et al., 2012).

Among UPPI states, we identified linkages between each lever (except leader tracking) and several others. Most notably, leadership standards is highly connected in that some UPPI states require licensure assessments, preparation programs, leader evaluation criteria, and/or professional development to align with state or national leadership standards. Licensure, program approval, and professional development are also very connected; we found evidence in UPPI states of these levers' complementarity with each other. For example, some licensure regulations specify requirements that candidates must meet prior to completing the program, and, often, sitting principals must satisfy certain professional development requirements to qualify for licensure renewal. Table 4.2 summarizes, for each lever, the number of other levers for which we observed any interconnectedness with other levers through all interviews or our document review. The table also identifies those interconnected levers and notes examples. These findings are in line with recent literature, which emphasizes that policy levers are rarely used in isolation.

Through our analysis of the use of the levers, we found that the interconnectedness between levers manifested in three main ways: (1) The use of one lever can reference or tie to the use of others, (2) a lever can draw authority from the use of another lever, and (3) changes in the use of one policy lever can trigger or require changes in the use of a different lever. In addition, we found that some examples of interconnectedness are more implicit than explicit; other examples are hypothetical, or are opportunities for state policy to create greater interconnectedness.

### Levers can be tied to or reference others

Interconnectedness manifests clearly when one lever references the use of another. For example, states often embed or reference standards in other processes and regulations through requirements or recommendations—whether licensure exams, program approval regulations, professional development systems, or evaluation criteria. As another example, program approval requirements might reference recruiting practices or licensure pass rates of candidates.

### Levers can draw on the authority of others

As noted earlier in this chapter, the use of a lever usually sits somewhere along the spectrum of influence, from information-sharing to guidance to inducement to mandate. A lever whose main mechanism of influence is information-sharing may be less able on its own to effect change in the behavior of stakeholders, since stakeholders may not be compelled to change to the same extent as for a mandate. However, we found that, by tying levers together, policymakers allow one lever to draw on the influence or authority of another, thus bolstering the impact of the first lever. As noted above, many levers reference the use of standards. Through that process of connecting standards to other levers, standards, which exist primarily as an information-sharing tool, draw on the authority of these other levers to effectively shift their position on the spectrum of influence. In states where standards-aligned licensure assessments or evaluation criteria are required, the standards themselves also become mandates.

**Table 4.2**
**Interconnectedness Among Policy Levers**

| Policy Lever | Number of Connected Levers | Examples of Interconnectedness |
|---|---|---|
| Standards | 5 | • States require **licensure** assessments to align to state or national leadership standards.<br>• State regulations require **programs** to align to leadership standards.<br>• States require leader **evaluation** processes to align to leadership standards.<br>• Standards are used to guide the **professional development** that principals receive; this may manifest through the induction programs that novice principals must attend, or the development of states' professional development systems.<br>• In **recruiting** candidates, preparation programs are likely to select candidates they believe are capable of meeting the competencies in leadership standards. |
| Recruitment of aspiring leaders | 3 | • **Licensure** regulations can dictate experience requirements or other prerequisites, which could influence who enters preparation programs.<br>• **Program approval** regulations require that preparation programs and districts collaborate in the candidate selection process.<br>• Connection to **standards** has been noted above. |
| Licensure | 4 | • Licensure regulations specify requirements that candidates must meet prior to completing the **program**.<br>• Regulations around licensure and licensure renewal specify requirements for sitting principals to complete certain kinds and amounts of **professional development.**<br>• Connections to **standards** and **recruitment** have been noted above. |
| Program approval and oversight | 4 | • In states with a two-stage licensure system and induction program embedded within the second stage, program candidates, who are novice administrators, receive **professional development** through their induction program.<br>• Connections to **standards, licensure**, and **recruitment** have been noted above. |
| Professional development | 4 | • Districts are required to use results of the **evaluation** process to inform principals' professional development goals.<br>• Connections to **licensure, program approval,** and **standards** have been noted above. |
| Evaluation | 2 | • Connections to **standards** and **professional development** have been noted above. |
| Leader tracking systems | 0 | N/A |

### Changes to one lever can trigger changes in another

Interconnectedness allows changes in one lever to trigger changes in another. For example, changes to the principal standards can trigger changes to program approval standards and, in turn, to licensure regulations. Depending on the magnitude of these changes, programs can also be induced or required to change their own practices and programming. This manifestation of interconnectedness allows states to create broader change by manipulating only one or a few policy levers; the more deeply interconnected a lever is, the more power it has to affect other facets of principal preparation.

### Additional opportunities to create interconnectedness are possible

We also found that additional types of interconnectedness are possible, though not yet realized within the seven UPPI states. Among the UPPI states, none had functioning statewide leader tracking systems, although there are plans to build statewide data systems with a focus on school leaders in North Carolina. As a result, we did not note any explicit interconnections between leader tracking and other levers. However, based on our review of Manna (2015) and leader tracking systems in other states, such as Ohio and Tennessee, there is potential for linking this lever with others, such as licensure, program approval, recruitment, professional development, and evaluation. For example, the Ohio State Department of Higher Education links data regarding preparation programs to evaluation data and to results of licensure exams. The state publishes a report annually and makes data available to districts and programs. The information provided by the state can help program candidates select the best program, districts select among principal candidates, and programs in their continuous improvement efforts.

## Factors That Can Influence the Effectiveness of Lever Use

Interviewees pointed to factors that they viewed as promoting or inhibiting the effective use of levers. For standards, there seems to be a recognition that simply publishing or adopting them does not lead to their use; concrete tools and supports, such as rubrics, help to make standards actionable. Standards also gain influence through their connection with other policy levers (as discussed above). According to interviewees, effective use of licensure as a lever is bolstered by a two-stage licensure structure and rigorous assessments. These help ensure that licensed principals have the depth and breadth of knowledge, skills, and experiences that they need to take on the role.

Meanwhile, licensure is a weak lever when alternative licensure routes do not include a requirement to complete a state-approved program, or when licensure assessments present a low bar. Interviewees said that the program approval and oversight lever is effective when the oversight agency has expertise and when the process is oriented around program and candidate performance and outcomes. On the other hand, it is difficult to use the lever effectively when state leadership standards are weak, when program approval is compliance-oriented, or when the state agency lacks capacity to enforce or oversee program approval standards.

Perhaps not surprisingly, funding is a key factor that promotes states' use of the professional development lever, as it enables them to provide programs accessible to principals statewide or those most in need of support (i.e., principals working in low-performing schools). Professional learning requirements based on counts of hours or credit completed, rather than the substance of the learning or skills gained, also inhibit effective use of the lever.

Finally, we heard from interviewees that clear state-level criteria or processes for evaluating principals support the effective use of the evaluation lever. Meanwhile, unclear or low evaluation criteria and district autonomy—allowing individual districts to establish criteria or thresholds and processes for evaluating its principals—inhibit effective use of this lever. Table 4.3 summarizes these facilitating and inhibiting factors by lever. These factors relate to some broader themes that we highlight below.

**Table 4.3**
**Factors State Interviewees Mentioned as Promoting or Inhibiting Effective Use of the Policy Lever to Promote Principal Quality**

| Policy Lever | Factors Promoting Effective Use | Factors Inhibiting Effective Use |
|---|---|---|
| Standards | • Concrete tools, such as rubrics, make standards actionable<br>• State-provided information, resources, and supports help with standards implementation<br>• Connection with other state policy levers | None |
| Recruitment of aspiring leaders | • State support for program participation | None |
| Licensure | • Two-stage licensure structure<br>• Rigorous assessments | • Alternative licensure routes that do not include state-approved programs<br>• Low standards (e.g., for passing licensure examination)<br>• Weak connection with program approval or standards lever |
| Program approval and oversight | • Expertise in oversight agency<br>• Performance and outcome-oriented metrics | • Lack of state capacity to enforce or oversee standards<br>• Low program standards<br>• Compliance-oriented<br>• Lack of standardized oversight process |
| Professional development | • Funding<br>• State-run or supported professional development programs | • Lack of funding<br>• Hour or credit-based requirements lacking in substance |
| Evaluation | • Clear state expectations<br>• Requirements for districts to submit evaluation plans to state | • District autonomy<br>• Low standards |
| Leader tracking systems | • Funding | None |

**Interconnectedness can enhance the complementary use of levers—for better or for worse**

Interconnectedness may promote the effective complementary use of policy levers to improve principal quality. This interconnected use can lend authority to policy levers that do not inherently embody authority. For example, standards can enhance the quality of the use of the program approval lever. As noted by one interviewee,

> I think [the standards are] clear. They are articulated. There's a continuum across the principals, you know the career spans. I think that they help you design the programs that allow them to demonstrate mastery of those standards so I think the standards are very helpful in articulating what people need to do and how programs can design around what they can do.

This finding is consistent with the literature. Capano and Howlett (2020) notes that policy instruments are often used in a mix or bundle, creating "interactive effects," which can either be complementary, counterproductive, or synergistic (Capano and Howlett, 2020, p. 2). "Complementary" instrument mixes "work together to support a policy strategy," and synergistic mixes are those in which different tools "taken together, are more effective than when deployed alone" (Capano and Howlett, 2020, p. 2).

Complementary, interconnected use of policy levers can amplify the impact of separate mandate-based policy levers by expanding the set of policy targets and reinforcing the underlying objective. Licensure, which primarily targets aspiring principals, and program approval and oversight, which primarily targets preparation programs, are strongly linked. In California, stakeholders were optimistic about the impact of the state's performance assessment on program quality because they believed the assessment would drive programs to ensure that their candidates obtain the knowledge, skills, and abilities they must demonstrate on the performance assessment. There are many points of connection among the standards, licensure, and program approval levers in this example. Both the assessment and program approval criteria are aligned to state standards. The assessment is required for program completion, which is in turn required for licensure; and the administration of assessment is also embedded within the state's program approval standards. This deep interconnectedness allowed the state to use both licensure and program approval levers such that they worked together (along with standards) to potentially improve both program and candidate quality throughout the state.

Interconnectedness can have a downside, however, when the implementation of one lever is weak. In our interviews, stakeholders who disagreed with or were neutral about the notion that their states effectively use licensure as a policy lever were skeptical about interconnections between the licensure system and program approval and oversight. Because the completion of a program is the primary licensure requirement in most states, stakeholders noted that when program oversight is weak and programs are not of high quality, the licensure process is weak. One stakeholder said,

> Anyone that graduates top of class or bottom—they're both licensed and can become principal. Nothing keeping them from getting proper certification. Someone may not have a leadership bone in their body, but they'll take classes and get the certification. . . . This person might graduate with someone that is a natural born leader. There's nothing separating them once they start classes at whatever university they're at.

Interviewees identified opportunities to enhance the complementary, interconnected use of levers in their state. One interviewee pointed out that there was no crosswalk between the state's leadership standards and the state's evaluation system. The stakeholder stated that such a connection would allow for more clarity for practicing principals. A stakeholder from a state that does not require the use of or provide a statewide principal evaluation tool, and that also does not require the use of its leadership standards in the evaluation process, noted that there was significant variation across the state in terms of the evaluation processes that districts implemented and the quality of those evaluation processes. Yet, this stakeholder found great value in being able to align the district's evaluation tool and components of the district's recruitment process to the state standards, thus also allowing for greater alignment between the district and preparation programs.

#### Two-stage pathways provide opportunities to use levers in an interconnected way

We observed that states with multi-staged leadership pathways have the opportunity to develop different sets of expectations for programs and principal candidates in each stage of the process. Indeed, stakeholders who agreed that their state effectively uses licensure as a policy lever often pointed to the two-stage feature of some licensure systems as a characteristic that promotes principal quality. With multi-stage licensure pathways, states can craft differentiated, more-targeted requirements for programs and candidates. For example, licensure assessments can be more targeted toward the candidate's stage in the preparation process, whether pre-service preparation or on-the-job training as a novice administrator. Program design can also be differentiated, allowing for targeted preparation for the state's licensure assessment. The multi-stage model also allows for overlap with professional development for novice administrators. In California and Georgia, the second stage of preparation was mentioned as providing candidates with a structured opportunity for more on-the-job training. One interviewee from California said, "The real work of the principalship doesn't start until you have the job and you step into the leadership role, which is the advantage of the Stage 2 credential. . . . The strongest development of leadership skills happens at the site level because the work is so context-specific." Where state pathways involve program participation in the second stage, those programs can effectively function as induction professional development, giving states more influence over professional development.

#### Evidence-based, rigorous requirements positively affect stakeholders' perceptions of a lever's effectiveness

When elaborating on states' effective use of a policy lever, interviewees often pointed to ways that evidence-based or rigorous requirements were embedded in the use of that lever. They emphasized that levers must be connected to high standards or evidence-based requirements in order to be effective; in comparison, requirements that were seen as simply "jumping through hoops," setting a low bar, or adding layers of bureaucracy were not seen as effective.

For example, some stakeholders we interviewed pointed to North Carolina's Transforming Principal Preparation Program (TP3), a competitive grant program, as effective because it requires participating programs to embed research-based elements into its programming. One such required element was the inclusion of a rigorous selection process, which was possible in part because the program provides candidates with a full-time paid residency by using state funds (BEST NC, 2018). Because of this selection process, stakeholders were more inclined to rate the state's efforts in recruiting aspiring principals as effective. As another example, California stakeholders were optimistic about a new competitive grant program to support professional development providers seeking to offer high-quality professional development for school leaders across the state. The state would select providers based on the alignment of their program to evidence-based practices. North Carolina and California are the two UPPI states that took the 3-percent state set-aside in ESSA, which requires that funds be directed toward evidence-based programs.

In contrast to their favorable perceptions of rigorous standards, interviewees were critical of state programs or requirements that they perceived to be oriented on compliance or "checking the box." For example, some stakeholders perceived that the licensure system in their state is not focused on the quality of one's work or one's abilities; rather, the process is mostly seen as hoops to jump through. One stakeholder remarked, "Our system is built to reward people who can endure a lot of meaningless preparation. And put up with and fulfill bureaucratic requirements. Not high talent that should be working with our kids." Interviewees noted that, perhaps as a result of this type of licensure process, their states have significantly more certified individuals than qualified individuals. Similar criticisms were lodged against the compliance nature of the program approval process in some states.

Across many levers, interviewees also pointed to instances in which the state had established a requirement that set too low of a bar for quality. This occurred with regard to licensure assessment, professional development, evaluation, and program approval. In the realm of program approval, interviewees mentioned that the approval criteria were not substantively connected to the quality of programs and allowed mediocre programs to operate and overproduce administrators that are not truly prepared to lead. An interviewee from another state that requires each district to provide a specific number of hours of professional development to principals described the state requirement as "paltry," saying, "It doesn't say what that PD [professional development] has to be offered in. I haven't seen [a] great deal of push, especially in the last couple of years around leadership PD or encouraging . . . superintendents to do leadership PD with principals." In another state, an interviewee noted that, at present, the state's evaluation instrument is "loose enough that administrators can get by."

**Programs and districts may need state support to meet rigorous state requirements**

Although stakeholders emphasized the importance of substantive, meaningful, and rigorous requirements in crafting policy, they also highlighted the notion that policymakers should also attend to the capacity of districts and programs to carry out these requirements. In particular, we observed that stakeholders perceived levers as more effective when state policymakers are sensitive to capacity constraints and thus design more-comprehensive policies that include both rigorous requirements and supports to carry out these requirements.

At times, even in the face of state mandates, the actual responsibility is left to districts or programs. If they lack the capacity to meet the mandate and are not given support to do so, even the most well-intentioned program or district may fall short of the requirement. In this case, the mandate—which might be well crafted and involve high standards—is still seen as not effective. For example, one interviewee mentioned that the state's requirement that preparation programs and districts form partnerships should—in theory—support recruitment; however, the rule "didn't operationalize well," particularly with regard to smaller districts.

When taking these considerations into account, we observed that states could bolster the effective use of rigorous, substantive, or evidence-based requirements by using these requirements in conjunction with other tools, such as support and guidance, which can then allow for a more comprehensive approach. The implementation of California's performance assessment is one such example; while the performance assessment required major changes to program practices, the state also provided support to programs through the implementation process through a variety of mechanisms, including office hours, virtual think tanks, convenings, and pilots of the assessment. These efforts were able to leverage insights from the state's participation in UPPI.

Similarly, funding was seen as an integral part of the success of North Carolina's TP3 and its ability to implement a rigorous selection process, especially given the difficulty of learning the complex job of a principal while either not being paid or concurrently working as a teacher. As one stakeholder said,

> When we've seen the state provide funding for people to go into principal preparation, and North Carolina is one of those states that has done that . . . when the

> state puts money forward and says it's important enough to us that we're going to somehow support people to be in principal programs . . . that's huge.

Speaking more generally about state policy, the stakeholder remarked,

> Again, I think you can have all the recruitment requirements you want, you better support that with some funding. It's just really hard for first-generation college people to come back for their master's and give up a portion of their salary to become an intern. So, I think the state needs to not just have requirements, but they also have to have some sort of financial support.

Additionally, in Georgia, stakeholders noted that the state has used a consistent evaluation tool for years, which is also mandated by law. Training on the evaluation tool, paid for by Race to the Top, has allowed for a deeper focus on evaluation in the state.

#### Lack of oversight, accountability, or resources impedes policy implementation and effectiveness

Stakeholders reported that the effectiveness of a lever diminished when the state did not exercise oversight to ensure that policy targets were meeting the policy intent or goal. One stakeholder commented on the state's approach to monitoring, mentioning that the "state has a pen and pencil approach to assessment and they monitor based on dimensions of whether [the program is] covering the content." The stakeholder continued by noting that the lack of oversight contributes to the ineffectiveness of the lever because the "[program approval lever] is not a lever for moving our 50th percentile programs into the 75th percentile or higher" since the absence of monitoring may remove an obligation of commitment by the programs. Furthermore, another stakeholder pointed out that even when there are laws, there is a lack of oversight ensuring that the requirement is being carried out. For example, there is legislation requiring districts to report to the state certain data that are relevant for preparation programs. That information is not, in fact, consistently reported to the state. The stakeholder expressed that, if states want to improve quality, they should, at a minimum, follow the requirements written in the legislation.

Interviewees and stakeholders also mentioned scarce resources as a challenge to the effective use of levers at all levels of policy implementation. States' ability to conduct oversight and accountability relies on the level of expertise at state agencies' and the agencies' capacity to fulfill those roles. A complex activity, such as holding programs accountable for implementing standards-based practices, requires both expertise and resources. Stakeholders in several states mentioned the importance of expertise in oversight, particularly in program approval. Stakeholders who felt that their state effectively uses program approval and oversight as a policy lever pointed to the efforts and expertise of the agencies providing oversight. For example, the California Commission on Teacher Credentialing has been working to improve principal preparation and oversight over programs through a range of activities, including measuring the performance of candidates against updated leadership standards and using the accreditation cycle to further implementation of California Administrator Performance Assessment results. Another interviewee also pointed out that when state agencies' budgets are cut, districts can only dedicate resources to state-identified priorities, which are often federally mandated programs, such as comprehensive school improvement.

## Conclusion

Ultimately, we observed tremendous variation across UPPI states in terms of which levers are used and how they are being used. One commonality across states was agreement that the standards lever was being effectively used to promote principal quality. All states used the levers in interconnected ways, but the levers that were connected in some states were not connected in others, and the mechanisms used in states to engender interconnectedness also varied. This variation among UPPI states demonstrates that states do have to actively craft policy to generate interconnectedness between policy levers, and that they have a number of available tools to do so, including mandates, incentives, and guidance and support. Our observations demonstrate the importance of considering how policy levers can work together in complementary and synergistic ways to promote policy goals and how the pathway to the principalship can be leveraged to allow for more nuanced use of policy levers.

CHAPTER FIVE

# Challenges to and Facilitators of Policy Change

In documenting the policies that UPPI states have enacted, we also learned about challenges to making (further) state-level progress in areas that support school leadership. Some of these provide insights into why states may have selected to activate the mechanisms that they did in effecting change. In the first half of this chapter, we describe some of the challenges we identified across states. In the second half, we identify and discuss possible facilitators that we believe contributed to states proposing or adopting change in an effort to improve school leadership statewide.

## Possible Challenges to Change

### Limited resources—funding, capacity, time—can constrain actions

A significant challenge to change is limited resources, a barrier that may often underlie an apparent preference for the status quo. With respect to financial resources, a few states (Florida, Georgia, and Virginia) did not take the 3-percent ESSA set-aside for school leadership activities specifically because they were aware that taking the amount meant a reduced flow of funds for school districts, which they felt needed such resources more.

Furthermore, in recent years, because of fiscal constraints, several states have had to cut funding to programs and initiatives that squarely supported leadership development in the state. Without adequate appropriations, it became difficult to initiate or sustain such work. In Connecticut, for example, a major initiative that provided one-year mentorship programs for aspiring leaders with residencies was terminated due to a state budget shortfall. As a result, the Connecticut State Department of Education was no longer able to support investments in leadership development efforts at scale directly, forcing the department to utilize grant-funded and partnership opportunities to support initiatives beyond those programs that are legislatively mandated.

Similarly, because of budget constraints, the Kentucky Principal Internship Program (KPIP) has not been funded since 2008, although the program remains in statute. The EPSB unsuccessfully tried to reestablish the funding for the program in 2017. The KPIP was designed to provide on-the-job experience to candidates who have completed a principal preparation program and received a provisional internship certificate. Upon completing KPIP, the candidate would be fully certified. With KPIP, no one would be fully certified as an administrator until they had completed this on-the-job training. It provides aspiring leaders and their future employers an opportunity to gauge whether the licensure candidates could be successful as a principal given their current skills.

Capacity limitations, especially during an austere time, also pose a challenge in multiple states. While a change may be well intentioned and agreeable, it could contribute to "initiative fatigue" and the sense that the change would lead to new work that individuals or agencies have little capacity to undertake. In the case of standards, for example, stakeholders may be inclined to argue that statewide adoption of new standards is unnecessary since the "new" standards simply reflect changes in wording, not in substance, particularly if the state had recently undergone standards revision or alignment. Underlying that argument is the idea that changing the standards would require changing other elements, including program approval and principal evaluation criteria. One state agency interviewee recalled that when a partner asked what legislation the agency intended to propose that year, the official had to tell them that the agency—particularly given recent downsizing and retirements—did not have the capacity to take on new laws and policies, however well intentioned: "We're pedaling as hard as we can. . . . At some point, we just have to stop all of the good ideas and all of the great well-intended policy and legislation." Included in the response was the sentiment that more support was needed to implement existing policy. The respondent reported thinking, "Do not propose any new things. Let's just join and help me pull the wagon on what we already have legislated and proposed as policy."

#### Low agenda status can relegate leadership issues to the backburner

School leadership often has low agenda status; it does not capture public or political interest to the extent that other education topics do. As a result, it can be difficult to bring reform ideas to the attention of relevant stakeholders and legislators, or such ideas may be quickly dismissed or pushed lower on the agenda. Rarely are issues of school leadership acted upon with urgency.

Speaking of a prior reform effort, one state interviewee reported that principal preparation was "not a shared value in the legislature. That's why it had difficulty getting traction. I would say it's not of high interest to [the] state board. A lot of political leaders have difficulty understanding why we need to do more than what's already going on." Another state interviewee noted that in a recent year, as the state agency was preparing to propose its legislative agenda to the commissioner and legislative liaison, she was asked to be "less prolific" in their request. She remarked that the commissioner and the liaison strategize about "priorities and using the political will and/or the political landscape. They make decisions [based on] what political will they [believe they] will have in a given session."

Issues related to school leadership often get rolled up in issues related to teachers, likely because teachers make up a much larger workforce. An interviewee who oversaw both teacher and school leader development in a state agency said as much, admitting that, because of resource constraints and the much larger number of teachers, he focuses more often on initiatives related to teachers. An interviewee from another state reported that, at the same time as there was a push for minority teacher recruitment, there was an effort to increase principal recruitment more generally, via interstate reciprocity. Instead of recognizing leadership recruitment as a distinct issue, it "ended up getting somewhat entangled with other [issues] around diversification."

Because of the lack of political backing, large-scale reforms and potentially effective but radical changes are not considered possible. One state interviewee expressed this in contrasting the approach their state is taking on principal preparation reform with that of Illinois in the 2010s, when the state shut down all principal preparation program providers and had each redesign their program and reapply for approval: "I wish in some ways that [what we are doing] was that bold, [but] it's not. . . . Without more pressure from upstairs [the commissioner and legislators], I'm not sure that we have as much ability because we're really not mandating any of this."

One possible reason for school leadership having the low agenda status and limited political support could be a lack of expertise about school leadership among key decisionmakers and those with political influence. A state interviewee serving in a leadership position for the state's efforts to support quality educators indicated that he simply was not aware of the research evidence on the importance of school leaders and how policy to support school leader development can serve state education policy. Through his work on UPPI, he became aware of the importance of school leaders. Similarly, in another state, an interviewee working at a nonprofit organization dedicated to school leadership development indicated that a primary aspect of the organization's work included educating state policy decisionmakers about the importance of school leaders and their role in providing quality education.

The folding of regulations for administrators into broader educator legislation made changes to those regulations particularly challenging. An entire regulation would need to be modified to address a specific aspect relating to, say, administrator certification in the state, potentially exposing a wide range of issues– including those concerning teacher certification, in this example—that the agency was not prepared to undertake. In response, state actors found ways to work around this barrier. For example, state interviewees noted that legislation could be crafted in a way that "supersedes" regulations. Grants are another way to move initiatives forward without having to go through legislation. A state official also noted that developing and distributing evidence-based practice guides was a way to nudge or guide district actions or "subtly put in place some requirements."

**Turnover of state leaders and political uncertainty can impede momentum**

Turnover of state leaders and general political uncertainty also delay or challenge policy changes related to school leadership. Such uncertainty may cause states to hesitate about proposing or enacting formal change because they do not know whether or how they may need to change course following an election. While an election may result in a state leader or legislature that is more favorable to educational leadership reforms, the unknown makes stakeholders more tentative.

Indeed, throughout fall 2018, with the midterm elections in view, interviewees from state agencies in states where the state commissioner of superintendent is appointed described being "in transition." They either anticipated or had just had a gubernatorial election, and some expected a new chief to be installed. During this time, when asked about potential regulation changes, one interviewee reported not knowing of any that were planned and could not predict the incoming governor's agenda or what the new commissioner or superintendent's priorities would be, or whether leadership development would be included: "That's always the issue. Which policies and initiatives will get really . . . embraced?"

Turnover in other key leadership positions in state agencies can also disrupt potential progress. Significant turnovers at the department of education in Florida prompted the School Educational Leadership Enhancement Committee Task Force (SELECT)—a body of stakeholders from the department of education, district leadership, academic researchers, and policymakers that was created to review school leader professional learning and supports in the state—to revisit their original recommendations and to create a revised version of their report to better reflect the priorities of the new administration and their preferred approach, which included deregulation. This led to some delay in the work, such as the release of a new report outlining updated school leader policy recommendations, although the state subsequently expressed more interest in significant legislative changes related to school leader policy, given the commissioner's support for such change.

In Kentucky, a political act temporarily changed the trajectory or timeline of some of the state's work. Governor Matt Bevin's 2018 executive order dissolved the EPSB and attached the board to the KDE in a newly established Office of Educator Licensure and Effectiveness for administrative purposes. The EPSB remained an independent board. The move was largely an operational and management one that did not alter the core authority of the former EPSB to pass regulations and issue certifications; however, the entire EPSB leadership turned over, and it took some time and effort to apprise the KDE of the ongoing work around improving principal preparation. In all, the move entailed a nontrivial amount of transition work that temporarily set back progress as adjustments were made with budgets and contracts. The EPSB remained a separate entity. The EPSB is appointed by the current governor, so new members were appointed to the board.

### In a context that values local control, states may be reluctant to "overreach"

Part of a state agency's calculation of whether and how to activate a particular policy lever involves considering what would lead to desired change through their targets of influence (e.g., program providers, districts). Even when states were determined to make a change, they were sometimes reluctant to do so because they did not want to appear to overreach their authority. This was particularly true in contexts that privileged local control.

In one state, a state-level interviewee was concerned that the absence of mandates requiring all state-approved programs to participate in reform-oriented activities would create or perpetuate "islands of excellence," wherein some programs prepared school-ready principals and others did not. The interviewee also admitted, however, that the agency had no ability or political will to require that institutions engage: "We don't do that. We are so low control. . . . We just don't have a big enough stick." In another state, officials have expressed a preference for using incentive-based approaches over mandates: "We . . . try to play a consistent role in incentivizing this type of investment in any potential way that can encourage it in a more organic way," as opposed to taking a mandate-focused, compliance-driven approach.

Perspectives reflecting this reluctance to mandate changes have held states back from taking action with respect to certain levers (e.g., certification, program approval, principal evaluation) or have nudged them to use softer mechanisms (e.g., incentives, support, information). For example, the Connecticut State Department of Education did not feel that it could tie program approval to the use of Quality Measures, and so, as described earlier, it offered small incentives in the form of grants to program providers willing to commit to engaging in Quality Measures and improvement planning for a two-year term. Similarly, the preference for softer mechanisms may have contributed in part to the wide use of convenings in many states to disseminate and build buy-in for promising practices (e.g., coaching of principal candidates).

In Kentucky, school-based decisionmaking (SBDM) councils have had the authority, pursuant to Kentucky Revised Statute (KRS) 160.345, to hire principals since 1990. KRS 160.345 does, though, grant the superintendent a vote in every principal selection process and establishes an alternative hiring mechanism whereby, if the council approves, the superintendent can recommend a principal candidate for the council to approve or deny. Additionally, since 2019, the selection of a principal in a county school district in a county with a consolidated local government adopted under KRS Chapter 67C (for example, Jefferson County Public Schools, which is Kentucky's largest school district) is subject to approval by the superintendent, who can select the principal if they do not approve the principal selected by the council.

Several recent legislative proposals have sought to further alter the principal hiring processes statewide but have been met with substantial resistance. Supporters in favor of SBDM councils continuing to make principal selections argue that teacher and parent voices are important in the matter and that the council's current role in principal hiring guards against superintendents wielding too much influence in school governance. Meanwhile, several key stakeholder groups argue that a superintendent is responsible for the operation and performance of all schools within the district; however, it is difficult or unfair for local boards of education to hold superintendents directly accountable for personnel (e.g., school principals) they did not have complete authority to hire.

## Possible Facilitators of Change

### Engaging stakeholders early and often can help states craft agreeable policy and facilitate buy-in

Stakeholder engagement greatly facilitated change related to school leadership policy across the UPPI states. In all states, there are existing and long-standing stakeholder groups linked to school leader issues that are typically brought into such policy discussions. These include the professional educator standards board—itself structured to ensure stakeholder representation (e.g., with representation from educators, school administrators, local board of education, higher education, and the private sector); state department of education; preparation programs; associations of principals, of superintendents, and of higher education faculty; regional education service agencies or cooperatives; and sometimes nonprofit organizations that advocate for or support school improvement. When major initiatives are rolled out, states leverage ongoing relationships with these entities to ramp up stakeholder engagement.

As one interviewee from a state agency explained,

> We've always worked with all the preparation programs in trying to look at are we meeting the needs [in this state]. . . . And we have a lot of people who offer professional growth opportunities for our principals, and so we have brought those stakeholders together with all of our preparation programs to try to facilitate, [asking] "What do we need in terms of guidance? What is it that everybody wants?" Facilitating discussion has been our role. We don't write regulations without input.

In the context of UPPI, the interviewee noted that a high level of stakeholder collaboration and strong relationships meant the state can move policies forward quickly: "We had the right people at the table to help us do that." Recognizing the importance of stakeholder engagement in making policy changes, an interviewee from another state identified a vision and mission of the agency as getting "better at engaging with partners. . . . How do we make sure that we have the stakeholders at the table, and that they are vested, and that they feel we are coming to them as partners in the work versus either trying to drag [them into] the work or do it in isolation?"

In addition, states have established structures—ad hoc committees and task forces—and invited stakeholder participation as they delved deeper and more comprehensively into school leader issues to explore policy actions. In those cases, the overarching idea has been to get a broad group of stakeholders together (including practitioners, academic researchers, and lawmakers) to make feasible, research-based recommendations to improve school leader policy) so that policy decisions are not made in silos. Such structures have further helped to build buy-in. Florida's SELECT, for example, was created to review school leader training and supports in the state. It brought together representatives from the Florida Department of Education, school district leadership, academic researchers, and school leader policymakers from around the state to focus on leader tracking, the leadership continuum, and alignment of Florida leadership standards to the PSEL. Similarly, North Carolina established the Principal Standards Committee, under the standing Professional Educator Preparation and Standards Committee (PEPSC), to evaluate the North Carolina principal standards relative to the PSEL. This committee's work led to a gap analysis between North Carolina Standards for School Executives and the PSEL, as well as recommendations to expand some standards (e.g., Micropolitical Leadership) and to include new ones (e.g., a standard on equity). In many, though not all, of these examples, resulting policies were adopted widely and smoothly because of the early involvement of stakeholders, whose early and continuous input helped to shape the policy, stem potential opposition, and secure the support of constituent groups. While these committees and stakeholder groups began ad hoc, some of these structures may sustain and become formal groups that convene regularly to discuss ongoing school leader policy issues.

**Leveraging stakeholders' expertise can help supplement and expand state capacity**

Beyond garnering buy-in for policies, engaging stakeholders has also facilitated change by expanding state capacity. As noted in the section on challenges, state agencies' resources and capacity are often limited. States leveraged other stakeholders' expertise to fill gaps in their capacity; they drew on organizations and individuals to help inform or disseminate state-level programs or decisions. For example, states learned from other states' policy efforts through UPPI professional learning community convenings. They also leaned into the universities participating in UPPI that are deeply involved in principal preparation program improvement. In both California and Florida, the state agency invited the UPPI university—San Diego State University (SDSU) and Florida Atlantic University—to participate in the development process of a state principal licensure assessment. Furthermore, all states positioned UPPI universities as experienced entities that other institutions could learn from. Among many examples, in Georgia, Albany State University's program redesign experience was featured in the new leadership strand of the annual state conference for educator preparation programs. Similarly, in Connecticut, at a state convening for districts and preparation program providers, the University of Connecticut shared a module it developed on family and community engagement for leaders. In Kentucky, the EPSB/KDE facilitated Western Kentucky University's sharing of its redesigned assessments and anticipates introducing other programs to Western Kentucky University's leader tracking system. And in California, SDSU supported change statewide through peer-to-peer dissemination by supporting 12 other university principal preparation programs to revise/redesign their programs in response to the California Administrator Performance Assessment with support from a grant.

State agencies also leveraged UPPI project leaders and teams' thinking on how to enable policy environments. In Florida, UPPI efforts helped pave the way to establish the SELECT to evaluate school leader standards and policy in the state, informed that task force's work across two administrations, and helped elevate school leadership for some Florida Department of Education leaders. Likewise, UPPI efforts in North Carolina expanded the idea of the leader tracking system from the district to the state level and informed the Principal Standards Committee's work to review the state's school leader standards.

Lastly, by identifying and inviting new stakeholders to serve on committees or participate in convenings, and by disseminating information about best practices and resources, state agencies have helped to build these other organizations' and individuals' knowledge, expertise, and agency with respect to school leadership issues. They are helping to grow the coalition of agitators and advocates for effective school leadership and policies that support such leadership.

These stakeholders are varied in kind and in role. In North Carolina, for example, the North Carolina Department of Public Instruction engaged BEST NC, a nonprofit, nonpartisan group of business leaders committed to improving the state's education system (BEST NC, 2017). BEST NC has maintained a singular focus on school leadership development in the state, directly lobbying state policymakers, providing influential reports on school leadership, and helping to establish the original TP3, which is now combined with the older NC PFP to serve as the state's umbrella principal preparation program. The competitive grants to preparation programs that use research-based best practices, established under the TP3, remain a key mechanism for improving principal preparation programs in the state and represented a shift in financial support of school leader quality by funding programs rather than aspiring principal candidates directly. While BEST NC's efforts appear to have increased the level of state support for leadership preparation, they may have shifted the focus away from more-traditional providers. States also engaged with districts as partners. In one state, one interviewee reported that school districts did not initially recognize their roles in principal preparation programs or the need to support matters related to program standards, accreditation, oversight, and other related policies. Upon participating in UPPI-related state-level discussions, however, superintendents realized that the regulations under discussion pertained to them as well. They learned that they were welcome and needed at the table, and, in turn, they were willing to contribute their perspectives. Similarly, in Connecticut, the state agency seized opportunities provided by UPPI-related meetings to learn about districts' school leadership needs, and then addressed those needs by developing and disseminating resources and hosting professional learning convenings for districts and program providers on topics such as equity-driven leadership. All told, across states, as districts and other stakeholder entities learn that their voice can promote change and that they have a role to play in influencing state policy, state agencies can leverage them to create change.

#### Low agenda status can be desirable

As described above, low agenda status can be a barrier to change, but interviewees also suggested ways that challenge might have a silver lining. As one state interviewee remarked, school leadership having lower agenda status means that there are not as many lobbyists against the issue, so proposed changes may not have to contend with as many challenges. Moreover, having a lower profile can help anchor (or lock in) any changes that are made. This is because when a governor champions an initiative, it can become a target and be easily replaced by other policies and priorities when that person leaves office. Lower-profile issues can be tackled in the background by professional bureaucrats, and resulting changes (to rules, legislation, etc.) can likely endure longer. One state agency interviewee interpreted the lack of deep involvement in leadership issues at the top levels as the leadership trusting them to move forward with what was needed; if lower agenda status meant less scrutiny around the work, it was welcomed. The extent to which the benefits of low agenda status outweigh the challenges it poses likely depends on the state context.

#### Leveraging related statewide efforts can help move school leadership efforts forward

Having to compete for attention with numerous other statewide education improvement efforts has been a challenge for school leadership, particularly regarding changes to higher education preparation programs. However, among the most significant examples of policy change we observed in UPPI states were efforts that built on or leveraged prior statewide efforts—focused on teachers or students, or on K–12.

Pushing for changes to school leadership policy as a follow-on to other statewide changes offers a number of practical advantages, which have been highlighted in the broader literature on agenda setting in policy reform (see, for example, Baumgartner and Jones, 2009). Advocating for changes to school leadership policy ties proposed policy change to broader state goals—for example, around equity or student achievement—which helps to argue for school leadership's relevance and urgency. In a number of states, equity—ensuring that every classroom has an effective educator—has been a major focus. Stakeholders agitating for change to policies involving school leaders have made the case for applying this principle to principals, as well. In a related example, one state interviewee said that the state's priority is less leadership as an end unto itself and more "leadership as a pathway to the improvement of schools." Within the department, there is an office dedicated to continuous improvement of schools—

and efforts that concern principals (as well as other educators) can be addressed within that priority. In other words, policies that improve principal preparation or development can be introduced as ways to ameliorate school culture and operations, enrich instruction, and ultimately improve student achievement and close achievement gaps. This has helped states get principal development to the table.

Using this strategy, states have connected and infused principal issues into multiple strands of work in different offices or divisions within the department of education: for example, offices focused on talent management, school turnaround, special education, and student performance. This distributive approach has helped to ensure that work on principal issues lives in various places, and policies cannot be ignored or undone wholly. Moreover, this approach buffers against capacity limitations. Departments struggling financially may not be able to or wish to devote an entire office or many staff to principalship issues. Spreading the effort among multiple offices or personnel and embedding in work already being done could be strategic and efficient.

In one state, it is not that issues regarding the principalship do not garner attention at all, but rather that when they do it is because of a direct tie to the K–12 system. This implies that issues related to licensure/certification, which seem most directly tied to preparation programs housed in higher education institutions, receive little consideration. Recent efforts to connect principal development in higher education to continued professional development of beginning principals have helped to elevate the profile of preparation programs and address some of their needs. In sum, the idea is that advocating for increased funding for or regulation changes regarding principals can be a steep hill to climb alone, but it is a much smoother and easier ride when hitched onto an engine that is already working its way up the hill.

Leveraging recent efforts focused on teachers, in particular, allows policymakers to make use of tested structures for policy change. In Florida, for example, major changes in teacher preparation programs enacted in 2013 provided a model for school leader legislation in 2015. In California, the California Administrator Performance Assessment was a follow-on to a teacher preparation assessment. Finally, in Connecticut, some of the recent efforts around leadership preparation (e.g., new administrator employer survey and Educator Preparation Program data dashboard) paralleled work completed for teacher education under the Educator Preparation Advisory Council before it phased out in 2016, leaving the proposed work around administrator preparation largely untouched. In essence, the teacher education reform paved the way, making proposed policy changes and activities related to leader development seem familiar to stakeholders—a natural next step—and less risky an investment. The work itself was often a lighter lift; language, templates, and processes used in teacher education improvement efforts—for example, for regulation changes or developing a survey or dashboard—could be repurposed or built upon.

### National policies and guidelines can be influential external drivers of change

External drivers can facilitate change by prompting deliberation of certain policy actions or providing needed resources. Specifically, national policies and guidelines in the form of ESSA, the PSEL, and CAEP accreditation standards have been influential.

The opportunity under ESSA for states to reserve 3 percent of their Title II, Part A, funding for school leadership activities directly prompted states to consider statewide efforts focused on improving or developing school leaders, even if they did not end up opting for the set-aside. The two UPPI states (California, North Carolina) that did take the set-aside have committed to using the funds to support the development of principals, for example, through state-offered programs that address essential leadership skills. It is unclear to what extent school leadership would have been a priority for these states without the ESSA impetus; however, exercising the option sends an unmistakable signal that principals are a key investment.

Similarly, the release of the PSEL motivated all UPPI states to reexamine their existing standards for school leaders, which involved performing cross-walks to identify potential gaps. In the end, five of the states adopted and/or adapted the PSEL as their state standards or considered doing so. On the whole, states believed it was advantageous to ensure alignment with the national standards (even if they did not formally adopt them) because the PSEL represented what was best known from research and real-life experiences about what effective principals need to know and be able to do; states did not want to lag behind. Instead, they wanted to be well positioned to have strong principals leading their schools throughout the state.

More important than the adoption of the PSEL are the policies and activities related to multiple levers that the PSEL led to. Once adopted or recognized as guideposts, for example, the PSEL motivated states to establish policies to improve principal preparation programs, reconsider the relevance and rigor of existing licensure assessments, and align principal evaluation standards with the PSEL. Such attempts at establishing coherence in principal development were greatly facilitated by the PSEL.

The CAEP standards are another national guideline that support change. Three UPPI states—Georgia, Kentucky, and Virginia—adopted CAEP's national accreditation standards for advanced-level preparation programs, leading them to emphasize certain criteria in program oversight or approval. For example, the standards mandate a strong internship requirement and district input into programs.

### Mandates, combined with supports or information, facilitate change

Mandates, of course, have the weight of authority behind them and, by their nature, can drive change. But implementation of mandates can be perfunctory or compliance-oriented. Implementers could resist the change, take exception to the top-down nature of mandates, or be genuinely unclear about how the change affects existing practice or unsure about how to implement the change. UPPI states have followed mandates with supports, in the form of information and/or training, and this combination of policy mechanisms seems to help induce change.

States that have adopted the PSEL, for example, have provided cross-walks between the PSEL and former state school leader standards or other relevant standards (e.g., principal evaluation standards) to help stakeholders understand the areas of overlap and highlight key differences, and provided conference/convening sessions with this focus. As mentioned above, when changing its principal evaluation framework, Kentucky provided a guidance document and will provide online modules to help principal supervisors understand and implement the standards as intended. Finally, in implementing the California Administrator Performance Assessment, the California Commission on Teacher Credentialing provided many opportunities for preparation program providers to obtain support (see Box 5.1). One interviewee noted that it would be difficult for the state to implement such a large-scale change without actively supporting programs through the change. In these and other instances, mandate-aligned supports are expected to help smooth the transition to the new policy and ensure strong take-up and implementation.

#### Offering resources or professional development with voluntary take-up of new policy or practice can also be a channel for change

In lieu of formal mandates or regulation changes, states sometimes offered resources (e.g., Connecticut's *Resource Guide for New Administrators* [Connecticut State Department of Education, 2018]) or professional development (e.g., offering preparation programs to engage with the Quality Measures program self-assessment tool; offering training on principal coaching or culturally responsive leading) that guided stakeholders in the direction of the desired change. Given the high take-up of these types of offerings across multiple states, this mechanism is likely especially effective for motivating change.

There are several reasons for this. Not using mandates can be interpreted as the state conveying respect for the autonomy and authority of the relevant entities to enact what they determine is necessary. Not using mandates also conveys an understanding of the capacity of the institutions by allowing them to determine whether a new policy or practice is feasible to implement. By offering voluntary take-up, states can focus on early, willing adopters and help them become successful. These early adopters can serve as examples or motivators for other sites. In Connecticut and Kentucky, for example, voluntary participation in the Quality Measures process began with a few institutions, then interest grew.

Supports are a much gentler mechanism than a mandate, as there are just about no imaginable negative consequences for accepting the support and trying out the policy or practice. In fact, states have made the supports enticing for target audiences—educator preparation programs and districts—as they are free or low-cost opportunities to enhance their programs and workforce. And as one state interviewee recognized, there are very few professional learning opportunities for principals, so the state can expect great interest in such offerings. The commitment is often low—for example, sending two faculty members or principals to attend a one-day training—and the potential yield is high, if the practice, when adopted, improves program delivery, candidate/ leader effectiveness, and student achievement.

Finally, although states may position new policies or practices as voluntary, program providers are likely to adopt them strategically, believing that they are designed to help them improve so they will be in a better position come program approval time. State interviewees have mentioned hoping that stakeholders would recognize the benefit of taking advantage of the state-offered resources or professional learning opportunities and that it may foreshadow formal policy in the future that they would be accountable to. In explaining why offering resources and professional development is an effective mechanism for change, one state interviewee alluded to a number of the ideas above, saying,

> We're trying to . . . provide for the administrator prep programs as much knowledge, skills, expertise as we can so they can take that and incorporate it into their programs. . . . We're hoping the motivation [for them] is, if [they] access what the [state] is offering at no cost to them, it will [have] impact down the road, so they'll be in a better position to have favorable results.

**Box 5.1**
**The California Commission on Teacher Credentialing Provided Information and Supports to Implementation of the CalAPA Mandate**

The California Commission on Teacher Credentialing (CTC) provided several layers of support to ensure a successful implementation of the California Administrator Performance Assessment (CalAPA). First, it provided numerous opportunities, both structured and less structured, for programs to collaborate with each other and also to connect with the CTC, through the use of weekly office hours, virtual think tanks, faculty training sessions, and conferences. Through these avenues, programs are able to ask questions, participate in discussions facilitated by the CTC and other stakeholders on the CalAPA's design team, and share best practices regarding the CalAPA's implementation.

In addition, the implementation of the CalAPA occurred in multiple phases. The CTC first fielded a pilot study in the 2016–2017 school year, in which 23 programs and 304 candidates participated, and then both surveyed candidates, program coordinators, and assessors, and conducted focus groups with candidates. Through these mechanisms, the CTC gathered feedback about how to improve aspects of the assessment as well as how to better support candidates and programs in its implementation. Following this pilot study and the revision of CalAPA over the summer of 2017, the CTC conducted a field test in the 2017–2018 school year. Following further revisions to the CalAPA, the CTC moved onto its next phase of implementation—an administration of the assessment that was nonconsequential for the purposes of licensure but required statewide for all candidates and programs during the 2018–2019 school year. Thus, even though the assessment was required, programs were given an additional year to review and revise their program offerings and prepare for the eventual consequential administration of the assessment. As a result, it was not until the 2019–2020 school year that the CalAPA became fully consequential (CTC, 2019b, 2020a).

CHAPTER SIX

# Conclusions and Recommendations

In this report, we have described the ways UPPI states use seven key policy levers to influence the quality of school leadership. We described examples of policy actions related to each lever and how those actions operate and provided examples of how states promote policy change. While the concept of comprehensive policy reform is compelling, the timeline and effort required to implement statewide policy reform—for example, efforts in Illinois to reform the state's approach on one lever, principal preparation—may be daunting to state leaders (see Hunt et al., 2019). In this chapter, we distill some key insights about states' targeted use of these levers that emerged from this review.

## Conclusions

### States promote principal quality through a range of policy actions

All states have access to levers that can improve school leadership policy. They use these levers to varying degrees, with different emphases and in different ways, to influence principal quality in the state. All states in our study have state-approved principal preparation programs and a pathway requiring participation in such programs—and program approval was a powerful lever in these states. Similarly, all states have leader standards and use them to inform actions related to one or more of the other levers. But there was substantial variation beyond these two areas. Our review of states' efforts did not identify a single "model" set of state policies to which all states should aspire. The right lever to pull, when to pull it, and how to pull it appear to depend on a range of contextual factors.

Our review of the use of levers indicated that standards, licensure, and program approval levers are actively used by all states. This is where the action is in terms of state policy influence on the quality of school principals. States also use the recruitment, evaluation, and professional development levers, at times leveraging the power of the licensure and program approval levers, but with more restraint. We did not find extensive evidence that the leader tracking system lever is currently being used, although there is interest in it among the states we studied.

Frameworks for promoting teacher effectiveness often include compensation and hiring practices as potential state policy levers. These topics came up in a limited way in our review. Among the UPPI states, North Carolina is the only state that has a statewide salary schedule. In other states, compensation is a district issue. While some interviewees mentioned low pay as a factor that could influence principal quality, there was no indication that the state would have much influence over this, except perhaps indirectly through education funding levels. Kentucky is the only state where we found any reference to a state role in hiring. There, state law assigns authority over a number of key decisions—including the hiring of school principals to SBDM councils rather than school districts. Under the 1990 Kentucky Education Reform Act, a school-based hiring committee consisting of at least two parents, three teachers, and the principal (per KRS 160.345) selects the new principal—meaning that the perspective of the superintendent may be overruled. Limitations to district hiring authority under this law, in turn, may have implications for the district role in recruiting aspiring leaders. In March 2019, Kentucky passed SB250, thereby removing the authority to hire principals from SBDM councils in Jefferson County Public Schools, the state's largest school district, instead vesting that authority with the superintendent. Shortly thereafter, in January 2020, SB7 was introduced, which would do the same across the state. As of the writing of this report, SB7 had passed the Senate committee and was proceeding to a second reading in the House committee.

**Use of levers is influenced by the principal pathway structure**

The state pathway to the principalship reflects policy choices related to the licensure lever. The structure of the pathway also defines opportunities for policy action related to school leadership. Five of the seven states we studied have a multi-stage pathway. Such a pathway provides states with an opportunity to use the licensure and program approval levers in more-nuanced ways. Licensure and program requirements can be tailored to the licensure stage to which the requirement applies. For example, the performance standards expected of candidates at stage 1 might be lower than for those at stage 2, reflecting an expectation of growth over time. Moreover, the pathway is not set in stone and can itself be the focus of policy change. A state can activate the licensure lever by adding a step to the pathway or adding a new requirement to a particular step of the pathway. The meaning and implications of specific licensure or program approval requirements must be understood in the context of the principal pathway for that state. For example, research suggests that high-quality preparation must involve clinical practice in addition to coursework (Anderson and Reynolds, 2015a). UCEA recommends that preparation programs include a minimum of 300 hours of clinical practice (Anderson and Reynolds, 2015a). In a state with a multi-stage pathway, such a recommendation could be met at one stage of the pathway but not the other or through a lower number of hours at each stage. This illustrates how policies must be tailored to the state's pathway to the principalship.

#### Use of levers is influenced by the constellation of state stakeholders and their roles

Although we identified a common set of key actors who influence state policy related to school principals across states, the relative influence of these actors varies by state. While such approaches can promote policy change quickly, they can also be readily undone after a change in administration. Although legislators have the formal authority to propose and pass legislation, state agencies implement legislation and often have substantial flexibility to influence how that implementation works. Finally, districts, associations, and other nonstate entities have substantial influence on both the legislative process and policy implementation. These on-the-ground stakeholders often identify opportunities requiring policy solutions and agitate for change.

#### Policy levers can be more effective when used in complementary, interconnected ways

We also found that the state policy levers are highly interconnected. This interconnectedness creates opportunities for the effective complementary use of policy levers to improve principal quality. Such interconnected use can lend authority to policy levers that do not inherently embody authority. For example, standards are most powerful when used as an alignment framework for licensure and program approval and oversight. Licensure and program approval and oversight are core authorities of states, and policy levers in this area are often implemented through mandates. We also observed examples of states leveraging that authority to influence evaluation and professional development through second-stage licensure requirements and/or licensure renewal requirements. Similarly, we observed states leveraging program approval requirements to influence recruitment and professional development. Although we did not observe any examples of states leveraging leader tracking systems through other policy levers in the UPPI states, such examples have been observed in other states.

#### States use mandates judiciously to influence principal quality

Although some studies have recommended that states be more active and directive when using their policy levers (Davis, 2016), there are trade-offs between promoting principal quality through directive mandates and allowing program or district flexibility. In addition, Manna (2015) advises against overly prescriptive program approval requirements that preclude innovation on the part of districts or programs.

Our review indicates that states tend to use mandates in areas where the direct policy target is an aspiring principal, principal, or program and where the mandate is attached to a privilege or benefit the state is conferring on the target—licensure to serve as a school leader or approval to operate a program. Even in these instances, mandates are coupled with or supplemented by information and supports. In the school leadership space, state actors appear to have a preference for less-directive approaches involving information with or without support. Where mandates are present, they tend to be accompanied by supports or exceptions. For example, flexibilities such as alternative pathways that allow candidates to bypass state-approved programs can diminish the influence of stringent licensure or program approval mandates, providing a safety valve of sorts that allows for local discretion. In some states, these alternative pathways are limited to individuals who have been hired by a district and recommended by their school district superintendent—deferring to local influence.

While mandates might appear to be the most powerful way for states to influence the quality of school leadership in the state, interviewees suggested a number of reasons why less-directive approaches might be preferred in certain circumstances. For example, the implementation of mandates can be perfunctory or compliance-oriented. Implementers could resist the change, take exception to the top-down nature of mandates, or be genuinely confused about how the change affects existing practice or unsure about how to implement the change. UPPI states have followed mandates with supports in the form of information and/or training, and this combination of policy mechanisms seems to help induce change.

Indeed, we found that states prefer to use policy actions grounded in information, resources, and supports, sometimes further enabled by incentives. This was a common way for states to influence school leadership across the state, and we observed numerous examples across policy levers. For example, states offered resources (e.g., Connecticut's Resource Guide for New Administrators [Connecticut State Department of Education, 2018]) or professional development (e.g., offering program providers to engage with the Quality Measures program self-assessment tool; offering training on principal coaching or culturally responsive leading) that guided stakeholders in the direction of the desired change. Given the high take-up of these types of offerings across multiple states, this mechanism is especially likely to be effective in motivating change while conveying respect for the autonomy and authority of the relevant entity to enact what it deems necessary.

#### States' use of policy levers reflects deference to local control

In education policy, there has been a long-standing preference for local control. State policy efforts may be viewed as an intrusion on that local authority. State policy actions focused on improving the quality of school principals will play out differently across the state, with different benefits and different costs in different settings. States have the opportunity to leverage their formal authority to prompt changes that could lead to more-effective principals in some locations, but they may choose not to or proceed with caution for a number of reasons, including deference to local autonomy. The degree of caution may be influenced by the degree of variation in local context within a state.

In reviewing examples of policy change, we observed that part of a state agency's calculation of whether and how to activate a particular policy lever involves considering what would lead to desired change through their targets of influence (e.g., program providers, districts). Even when states were determined to make a change, they were sometimes reluctant to do so because they did not want to appear to overreach their authority—especially in contexts that valued local control.

#### Low agenda status can inhibit but also facilitate statewide change

School leadership often has low agenda status. It does not capture the same degree of interest from the public as other education topics or priorities do. This can make it difficult to get legislators or other policymakers to act on the ideas. At the same time, the low agenda status of school leadership can be desirable. A lower profile can help an issue get through the policy process and help anchor changes that are made—making them less vulnerable to being overturned.

This suggests that efforts to move school leadership to the center of the policy agenda may be counterproductive and make initiatives more vulnerable. Instead, we observed that state policymakers were able to promote substantial changes by picking and choosing specific initiatives that could be tied to higher-priority education policy issues such as teacher preparation or equity or could leverage initiatives that had been successfully implemented for teachers or other educators.

## Recommendations

Our research surfaced a number of examples of UPPI states implementing policies and activities to impact the quality of school leadership using each of the seven levers. We identified several factors that appear to facilitate policy change. Chief among them is careful consideration of the mix of policy options available and the connections among levers. Early and meaningful engagement of stakeholders helps to ensure the crafting of an agreeable policy that will garner buy-in and helps to expand state capacity. Mandates are a powerful way to drive policy change but appear to be most effective when combined with supports and resources to support the state's desired changes in the behavior or perspective of policy targets. Low agenda status and leveraging related statewide efforts can help move and sustain policy efforts.

#### When setting policy priorities to improve principal quality, consider the mix of policy options available

Because the state policy levers are interconnected and their use is influenced by the state's pathway to the principalship and other aspects of the state context, there is no one-size-fits-all approach to revising state policy to improve principal quality. States should consider whether there are ways to leverage or enhance existing mandates by linking them more strongly to principal standards and to one another and associating them with rigorous expectations. The fact that different policy levers have greater or lesser influence at different points along the pathway to the principalship means

**Considerations for States Interested in Improving School Leadership Statewide**

- Consider the mix of policy options available and how existing mandates can be leveraged or enhanced.
- Build state-level engagement and expertise on principal quality.
- Couple mandates with information, resources, and support.
- Be opportunistic: Link principal initiatives to state education priorities and existing initiatives.

that consistent and aligned use of different levers can promote a coherent state strategy for improving principal quality.

### Identify opportunities to build stakeholder engagement and state-level expertise on principal quality

The education policy literature has raised concerns about the limited capacity of state education agencies, due to their increasing responsibilities, budgetary pressures, and the tendency for states to prioritize local over state resources. But state education agencies do not define state capacity. There is a wide range of other entities that influence legislation, advise on implementation, and serve on task forces and panels. In each state, there are formal (sometimes required) and informal opportunities for influence. UPPI states provide examples of the range of entities that can exert such influence.

Stakeholder engagement is central to many of the examples of successful policy implementation and policy change highlighted in this report. States leverage ongoing relationships with key stakeholder groups when key initiatives are rolled out or changes are being considered. These include professional standards boards, which are structured to ensure stakeholder representation (e.g., with representation from educators, school administrators, local boards of education, higher education, and the private sector); the state department of education; educator preparation programs; associations of principals, superintendents, and higher education faculty; regional education service agencies or cooperatives; and, sometimes, nonprofit organizations that advocate for or support school improvement. These stakeholder groups can be leveraged in a variety of ways and effectively expand the state's capacity.

Other stakeholder groups can also be drivers of policy change. States can support or amplify organic efforts by providing a forum or mechanism for information-sharing (such as professional learning community meetings, think tanks, or convenings). In addition, by identifying and inviting new stakeholders to serve on committees or participate in convenings, and by disseminating information about best practices and resources, state agencies can help to build other organizations' and individuals' knowledge, expertise, and agency with respect to school leadership issues. These other organizations, in turn, are helping to grow state capacity to advocate for effective school leadership and policies that support such leadership.

#### When using state mandates to drive principal quality, couple them with information, resources, and supports

Mandates regarding licensure, evaluation, and program approval requirements can be a powerful way for a state to drive improvement to principal quality. But when using such approaches, states need to be sensitive to the capacity of the policy targets to live up to those mandates. When the policy is targeting changes in the behavior of aspiring principals, principals, districts, or programs, it will be effective only if those actors can meet the expectations of the policy. Coupling mandates with resources and information to help develop that capacity—by funding programs with state resources, promoting peer networks, and developing information resources that stakeholders can tap—can increase the odds of success. Policymakers also must consider the evidence base when imposing mandates and consider removing requirements that are not achieving the desired aim.

#### Be opportunistic: Link principal initiatives to key state education priorities and build on related initiatives

Among the most significant examples of policy change we observed in UPPI states were efforts that build on or leverage prior statewide efforts focused on teachers or students, or on K–12 education. In addition, we observed examples in which external drivers, such as new national policies or guidelines, facilitated change by promoting consideration of policy actions. This suggests that state actors should be opportunistic in developing policy initiatives focused on principals. Rather than design a proposal from the ground up, stakeholders should scan the state landscape for significant policy efforts focused on teachers and consider whether and how something similar might be developed and implemented with a focus on principals. In a sense, this approach capitalizes on low agenda status as a way to efficiently promote policy change related to school principals. After a state has invested resources to develop a performance assessment for aspiring teachers or an evaluation tool for current teachers, building from that base to develop a similar tool for principals may be relatively feasible compared with an effort that needs to be developed from scratch. A related strategy is to tie or frame an initiative with reference to another high-level state or national initiative. In other words, states should be strategic and opportunistic in choosing which lever to pull, given the interconnectedness of policy levers.

## Final Thoughts

Since 2016, UPPI states have collectively implemented a range of policies and activities to improve the quality of school principals using each of the seven levers. In doing so, states have met considerable challenges, including capacity and fiscal limitations that constrain the ability to prioritize school leadership as an agenda item. Issues of local autonomy and stakeholder and constituent buy-in also influence the policies that states put forth and the mechanisms—combinations of mandates, incentives, supports—they use. Several factors do appear to facilitate policy change. Chief among them is early and meaningful engagement of stakeholders, which helps to ensure crafting of an agreeable policy that will garner buy-in, and which helps to expand state capacity. Low agenda status and leveraging related statewide efforts can in fact help move and sustain policy efforts. Mandates combined with supports, and offering resources or professional development with voluntary take-up of new policy or practice, appear to be preferred mechanisms for change. Stakeholders repeatedly pointed to coherent use of evidence-based policies as contributing to effectiveness. Our review highlights that the evidence base more often points to flexible practices, such as university-district partnerships or performance-based assessments, than rigid requirements, such as a specific number of clinical practice hours or content-oriented assessments. In future work, we plan to track these changes and explore the implications for principal preparation programs.

APPENDIX A

# Methodology

## Data Sources

We drew on three key data sources for this report: interviews with UPPI university-based leads and state partner leads, interviews with additional state-level stakeholders, and secondary data.

### Interviews with UPPI University-Based Leads and State Partner Leads

First, we drew on data collected from seven rounds of visits to UPPI sites, conducted in spring and fall 2017–2019 and spring 2020. Combined across the seven UPPI sites then, we conducted 49 site visits. Specifically, for this study, we included hour-long interviews with the university-based lead at a UPPI site (n = 51 interviews total over seven site visits) and the lead(s) at the state partner institution (n = 54 interviews total over seven site visits). Table A.1 summarizes the interview data we collected for this report.

### Interviews with Additional State-Level Stakeholders

Second, between April and July 2019, we conducted 47 additional interviews with state-level stakeholders across the seven UPPI states (see Table A.1). We conducted the 45–60-minute interviews by phone or, when possible, in person during our spring 2019 site visits. Interviewees were identified using a snowball sampling method that included recommendations from UPPI university-based and state partner leads. Interviews we conducted were with stakeholders in six main roles: representatives from state government (n = 4 interviews across seven states); state department of education or professional standards boards, beyond UPPI state leads (n = 6); educational cooperatives or county offices (n = 6); districts or related associations (n = 15); university faculty or administrators, beyond UPPI university-based leads (n = 8); and nonprofit or advocacy organizations (n = 8). To guard against potential breach of confidentiality by inference, we do not identify the number of participants by role by state.

Note that we invited more stakeholders than participated in the interviews. As Table A.2 shows, across states, we reached out to 19 more potential interviewees across a range of roles. For various reasons, however, these interviews were not conducted

**Table A.1**
**Interviews That Informed This Analysis**

| | Number of Interviews | | | |
|---|---|---|---|---|
| State (UPPI University) | With UPPI University-Based Leads (Spring and Fall 2017–2019 and Spring 2020) | With UPPI State Partner Leads (Spring and Fall 2017–2019 and Spring 2020) | With Additional Stakeholders (April–July 2019) | Total |
| California (San Diego State University) | 7 | 7 | 12 | 26 |
| Connecticut (University of Connecticut) | 7 | 10 | 3 | 20 |
| Florida (Florida Atlantic University) | 7 | 10 | 5 | 22 |
| Georgia (Albany State University) | 7 | 8 | 4 | 19 |
| Kentucky (Western Kentucky University) | 7 | 7 | 8 | 22 |
| North Carolina (North Carolina State University) | 9 | 7 | 10 | 26 |
| Virginia (Virginia State University) | 7 | 5 | 5 | 17 |
| Total | 51 | 54 | 47 | 152 |

**Table A.2**
**Number of Planned Additional Stakeholder Interviews That Were Not Conducted, by State and by Role Across States**

| State | Number |
|---|---|
| California | 2 |
| Connecticut | 4 |
| Florida | 2 |
| Georgia | 3 |
| Kentucky | 1 |
| North Carolina | 3 |
| Virginia | 4 |
| Total | 19 |

| Role | Number |
|---|---|
| State government | 0 |
| State department of education or professional educator standards board | 6 |
| Educational cooperatives or county offices | 0 |
| Districts or related associations | 4 |
| University faculty or administrators | 5 |
| Not-for-profit or advocacy organizations | 4 |
| Total | 19 |

(e.g., invitees declined or could not be reached after multiple attempts). In the end, then, we conducted 71 percent (47/66) of the planned interviews with additional stakeholders. While we would like to have spoken with more representatives and at least one representative in each role in each state, our sample of additional stakeholders ultimately depended in large part on the UPPI university-based leads and their role in brokering an interview for us.

### Secondary Data

Our third key source consisted of relevant secondary data, such as state ESSA plans, state licensure requirements, state legislation, reports from state departments of education about topics related to any of the key policy levers, and research literature on school leadership.

## Interview Topics

### Interviews with UPPI University-Based Leads and State Partner Leads

In each round of site visits, interview questions with UPPI university-based leads and state partner leads were focused on the roles and responsibilities of organizations and individuals involved in state-level school leadership efforts, state policy context and changes in the context that may affect work around school leadership, state agencies' engagement with principal preparation program improvement at the grantee institution and across the state, and facilitators and challenges to engaging in work to improve the quality of school principals across the state. Table A.3 shows sample questions on these main topics. Responses to these and related questions informed the findings throughout this report, with the notable exception of the Chapter Two section on what stakeholders had to say about the use of each of the policy levers.

### Interviews with Additional State-Level Stakeholders

In the interviews with additional state-level stakeholders, we asked about the agenda status of school leader preparation in the state, state policy context, policy changes related to school leadership, and the extent to which they agreed (on a 4-point scale of Strongly Disagree/Disagree/Agree/Strongly Agree) that their state uses each of the seven policy levers we were interested in effectively to influence principal quality. Table A.4 provides the key questions in the interview for additional state-level stakeholders.

Data for the Chapter Three section on what stakeholders had to say about the use of each of the policy levers derived from the last set of questions. In the spring 2019 interviews, five UPPI university-based leads and eight UPPI state partner leads also responded to this set of questions about the state's use of the levers. In total, then, we had 60 interview responses to the levers questions to analyze (13 from UPPI leads and 47 from additional state-level stakeholders). See Table A.5 for a summary of the data collected on this specific set of questions.

**Table A.3**
**Sample Interview Topics and Questions for UPPI University-Based Leads and State Partner Leads During Each Site Visit**

| Topic | Questions for University-Based Leads | Questions for State Partner Leads |
|---|---|---|
| Roles and responsibilities | • What state-level organizations have been involved in UPPI? | • Which individuals in various state-level organizations have been involved in UPPI, and in what capacity?<br>• Have there been personnel transitions within the organization that affected the UPPI work? Explain and describe how transitions or turnovers were handled. |
| State policy context and changes | • Since our last visit in, has anything changed at the state, regional, university, or district level that may affect school leadership development? If so, briefly describe the event or change. | • Since our last visit in, has anything changed at the state level that may affect school leadership development? If so, briefly describe the event or change.<br>• Have there been any changes in general availability of resources—financial, human, or other—that affect the work? |
| State agency's engagement | • How has the state partner engaged in your university's program redesign process?<br>• What principal development work has the state partner engaged in? How, if at all, has this work influenced the landscape of school leadership? | • How have you and your organization engaged in UPPI work?<br>• How have you engaged other programs or organizations across the state in principal preparation program improvement?<br>• Has the UPPI work led to discussions or engagement with officials in other state-level organizations about policies or structures that influence school leader preparation? If so, please explain. |
| Facilitators and challenges | • What factors help keep the UPPI work on track or propel the work forward?<br>• What factors make it difficult for you and/or people on the UPPI team to engage? | • What factors help keep the UPPI work on track or propel the work forward?<br>• What factors make it difficult for you and/or people on the UPPI team to engage?<br>• What lessons learned or advice would you offer to state organizations supporting principal preparation program redesign or related work? |

## Coding and Data Analysis

### Open-Ended Interview Data

We generated detailed notes or transcriptions of all interview data, then coded and analyzed these in Dedoose (Dedoose, 2018), a cross-platform internet application that assists with qualitative data.

The key top-level codes we generated to analyze the interview data from UPPI site visits and additional state stakeholder interviews corresponded to the main interview topics. The codes included "Agenda Status"; "State Context," which included

**Table A.4**
**Sample Interview Topics and Questions for Interviews with Additional State-Level Stakeholders**

| Topic | Questions |
|---|---|
| Agenda status | • Currently, what are the top three state education priorities? How does school leadership fit into state education priorities? OR Can you tell me why you think school leadership is a priority for the state? |
| State context | • Historically, what has been [your organization's] role with respect to influencing/shaping principal preparation and development?<br>• Are you (yourself) involved in principal preparation initiatives or programs in general? If so, how are you involved? What other departments/divisions within your organization may be involved?<br>• What other organizations are involved in such support? How do they work together?<br>• If someone wanted to move the needle on school leadership, who would be, or should be, at the table to make that happen?<br>• How do education programs/priorities/laws get changed in [state]? How is [your organization] involved in making those changes? |
| State policy changes | • Have there been any recent changes or events (e.g., policies or initiatives) at the state level that impact principal preparation that you think are important or notable? Please describe these changes, and comment on the drivers. |
| State use of policy levers | • Given the scale of Strongly Disagree-Disagree-Agree-Strongly Agree, how would you rate the following statements. Please briefly explain your rating. "State-level efforts with respect to . . . are effective in promoting principal quality in this state."<br>...leadership standards<br>...recruiting aspiring principals<br>...approving and overseeing principal preparation<br>...licensing principals<br>...supporting principal professional development<br>...evaluating principals<br>...leader tracking<br>• In which of these areas do you think [your state] is an exemplar? Why?<br>• In which of these areas do you think [your state's] efforts are most in need of improvement? Why? |

sub-codes to capture mentions of institutional policies and structure, resources, and relevant initiatives; "State Policy Change"; "State Partner Engagement" in UPPI; and factors that challenge and support efforts to influence school leadership in the state. We applied multiple codes to an excerpt as relevant. We followed established qualitative research procedures for ensuring reliability in our coding process (Denzin and Lincoln, 2003; Lincoln and Guba, 1985; Miles and Huberman, 1994; Strauss and Corbin, 1994).

Our team of four coders and two senior researchers met to establish an initial coding scheme, define the codes, and train on the coding scheme. A primary analyst coded the data for each site (i.e., state). A second analyst/researcher sampled transcripts to conduct an informal reliability check. We held occasional meetings and had impromptu exchanges to discuss and resolve ambiguities and discrepancies. We revised the coding scheme and documented decision rules, as necessary.

**Table A.5**
**Number of Interviews Conducted with Levers Questions, by State and by Role Across States**

| State | Number |
|---|---|
| California | 15 |
| Connecticut | 4 |
| Florida | 8 |
| Georgia | 4 |
| Kentucky | 10 |
| North Carolina | 11 |
| Virginia | 8 |
| Total | 60 |

| Role (Number of UPPI States Represented) | Number |
|---|---|
| State government (4) | 4 |
| State department of education or professional educator standards board (6) | 14 |
| Educational cooperatives or county offices (3) | 6 |
| Districts or related associations (7) | 15 |
| University faculty or administrators (5) | 13 |
| Not-for-profit or advocacy organizations (5) | 8 |
| Total | 60 |

Drawing on Strauss and Corbin (1990), we consider themes (or "categories") as "conceptual labels placed on discrete happenings, events, and other instances of phenomena." Themes are the classification of more discrete concepts and are "discovered when concepts are compared one against another and appear to pertain to a similar phenomenon" (p. 61). We drew on established techniques (Bernard, Wutich, and Ryan, 2016; Ryan and Bernard, 2003) to identify themes, including looking for repetitions, similarities and differences between sets of data (e.g., multiple interviews with the same respondent, different respondents in the same state, or across states).

Our analysis of interview data and identification of potential themes drew on two approaches. We identified themes a priori based on literature and analysis performed for our UPPI implementation report (Wang et al., 2018). We also identified themes through an emergent process that included several data reduction and synthesis processes. First, immediately after each site visit, the two data collectors worked together to complete a summary sheet for each interview. The sheet captures the agreed-upon key takeaways and potential themes. The summary sheets guided the debrief of the site visit with the full project team. During such debriefs, the team identified and discussed potential emergent cross-site (i.e., cross-state) themes, drawing on data from past site visits. We kept a record of emergent themes in a spreadsheet. In addition, we conducted a systematic review of coded excerpts relevant to the state report to verify themes we identified in the processes described above and to identify additional themes. We did so in a process described as "cutting and sorting" by Ryan and Bernard (2003). Specifically, guided by the research questions for this report, we ran multiple relevant queries on key codes. Two trained qualitative analysts read through all excerpts returned by the query for each site (i.e., state). As they did so, they "cut" out and summarized the ideas in relevant excerpts in spreadsheets. Each column of each spreadsheet represented a UPPI state, and each row represented a theme or finding. After all excerpt ideas had been captured on the spreadsheets, the full project team examined the sheets to conduct a "validity" check on the analysts' understanding of the excerpts and issues described and to "sort" the cells independently, suggesting ideas (e.g., examples of policy changes, barriers) that "go together" (i.e., that suggest a theme). In team meetings, we formalized these themes. Subsequently, we generated analytic memos summarizing the themes.

We took multiple steps to ensure the integrity of our findings. As mentioned above, we used multiple approaches to identify emerging themes or "pattern codes" (Punch 2014), including completing site visit summary sheets, keeping a running record of potential themes, systematically reviewing all relevant coded excerpts, and engaging in team debriefs and biweekly analysis meetings. Throughout the analysis, we sought both confirmatory and disconfirming evidence and triangulated data across sources, time, and researchers (Denzin, 2006). Finally, we conducted fact-checking; we made the sections of the report that explicitly referenced specific states and state organizations available for UPPI state partner leads to review for accuracy.

### Data on State Use of Policy Levers

Specifically, for the question about the state's use of each of the seven policy levers, we conducted several analyses. First, to examine the extent of consensus within-state, we recorded all the responses in a table, where each row represents a lever, each column represents a respondent, and the cell content represented their rating on the strongly agree to strongly disagree scale. We then reduced the data into four categories: strongly agree and agree collapsed together, strongly disagree and disagree collapsed together, neutral (although this was not a response option, several interviewees provided this response), and "I don't know" or no response. We tabulated the number of responses in each of these categories. Then the two team members responsible for each site identified areas of convergence and divergence based on the tabulation. Team members also summarized respondents' narrative responses for their rating.

The data reduction tables and summaries were subsequently shared with the full project team for cross-state observations of patterns.

We also analyzed responses to the question about the state's use of each policy lever by respondent role. As mentioned earlier, we identified six main roles—representatives from

- state government, including legislators and representatives from the governor's office

- state departments of education or professional standards boards, including the commissioner or state superintendent of education, state board of education representatives, and UPPI state partner leads
- educational cooperatives or county offices
- districts or related associations, including state associations of school administrators
- university faculty, including UPPI university-based leads, faculty association representatives, and university administrators, including deans and provosts
- not-for-profit or advocacy organizations.

First, we took the full response table for each state generated in the above analysis and reduced the data. Where there were multiple respondents in each role, we took the modal response, not counting the "I don't know" or no response category. Then we tabulated the number of responses in the strongly agree/agree category and the strongly disagree/disagree category. Because respondents were asked to rate the perceived effectiveness of each lever in promoting principal quality *in their state*, comparing by role across states is not appropriate. Instead, we examined results across roles within-state for each of the seven states for patterns.

### Secondary Data

To process the documents about state policies and context, we read through the documents we collected and synthesized relevant information in drafts of state profiles featured in Appendix B. An outline with key questions guided our synthesis. These documents were used to triangulate interview reports of how states used various policy levers and efforts to enact policy changes.

## Limitations

The data have several limitations. All interview data were self-reported by respondents. As a result, they reflect individual perspectives; they were not independently verified. Also, while we have confidence that all interviewees were key stakeholders or represented key state-level organizations, we did not interview all possible key stakeholders or organizations. We relied on UPPI leads to help identify key stakeholders, and although we made multiple attempts to interview all recommended stakeholders, there were some who did not participate in an interview. In this respect, our interviewees represented a convenience sample, and our participants may not represent all possible participants' perspectives. Third, the generalizability of the study findings is limited. As noted in the report introduction, by electing to participate in UPPI, these states may differ from the other 43 states. In fact, each of the states was deemed to have a policy context supportive of high-quality principal preparation, which cannot be said of all the other states.

It is difficult to say in which direction the findings we present (for the opinion-based question about the effectiveness of state efforts to use various levers) may be affected given these limitations. On the one hand, it is possible that respondents provided more positive views of their state's efforts to align with socially acceptable views and appear less negative or critical, or because they have been involved in initiatives (including UPPI) or some policy changes directly. Thus, from their perspective, progress is being made. On the other hand, working in the field or having a stake in it could enable one to more clearly see areas needing improvement; respondents may be more aware of "what else" is needed to improve principal quality and therefore be inclined to view current state efforts as inadequate. In general, we can imagine that those who accepted our invitation to be interviewed likely have strong views—favorable and unfavorable—on principal quality and development in their state.

APPENDIX B

# State Profiles Overview

In the state profile appendix, available at www.rand.org/t/RRA413-1, we provide a profile of the use of policy levers for each of the seven UPPI states. The profiles provide a way for interested readers to understand the use of individual policy levers in a broader context and highlight examples of interconnectedness. Each profile addresses the following:

- the state context: key players and their roles, including a discussion of key non-state entities involved in principal policy in the state
- the agenda status of school leadership in the state
- the use of each of the policy levers:
  - leader standards
  - recruitment of aspiring leaders
  - principal licensure and program approval and oversight, including a description of the pathway to the principalship in the state
  - professional development
  - evaluation
  - leader tracking systems.

These summaries are based on a review of publicly available information, as well as information obtained from interviews when it can be reported in an unidentifiable manner.

# References

Anderson, Erin, and Amy L. Reynolds, *A Policymaker's Guide: Research-Based Policy for Principal Preparation Program Approval and Licensure,* University Council for Educational Administration, 2015a. As of September 6, 2020:
http://3fl71l2qoj4l3y6ep2tqpwra.wpengine.netdna-cdn.com/wp-content/uploads/2014/05/UCEA-State-Policy-Report-website-version-Nov2015-v2.pdf

Anderson, Erin, and Amy L. Reynolds, "The State of State Policies for Principal Preparation Program Approval and Candidate Licensure," *Journal of Research on Leadership Education*, Vol. 10, No. 3, 2015b, pp. 193–221.

Anderson, Leslie M., Brenda J. Turnbull, and Erikson R. Arcaira, *Leader Tracking Systems: Turning Data into Information for School Leadership,* Washington, D.C.: Policy Studies Associates, Inc., 2017. As of September 6, 2020:
https://www.wallacefoundation.org/knowledge-center/Documents/Leader-Tracking-Systems-Turning-Data-Into-Information-for-School-Leadership.pdf

Augustine, Catherine H., Gabriella Gonzalez, Gina Schuyler Ikemoto, Jennifer Russell, Gail L. Zellman, Louay Constant, Jane Armstrong, and Jacob W. Dembosky, *Improving School Leadership: The Promise of Cohesive Leadership Systems,* Santa Monica, Calif.: RAND Corporation, MG-885-WF, 2009. As of September 20, 2020:
https://www.rand.org/pubs/monographs/MG885.html

Baumgartner, Frank R., and Bryan D. Jones, *Agendas and Instability in American Politics, Second Edition*, Chicago, Ill.: University of Chicago Press, 2009.

Bell, Liz, "New Commission Works on Teacher Preparation Guidelines, Standards," EdNC, November 10, 2017.

Bernard, H. Russell, Amber Wutich, and Gery W. Ryan, *Analyzing Qualitative Data: Systematic Approaches*, Thousand Oaks, Calif.: SAGE Publications, 2016.

BEST NC—*See* BEST NC: Business for Educational Success and Transformation.

BEST NC: Business for Educational Success and Transformation, "Statement from BEST NC on Principal Pay," 2017. As of May 1, 2020:
http://best-nc.org/statement-from-best-nc-on-principal-pay/

BEST NC: Business for Educational Success and Transformation, *Transforming Principal Education in North Carolina: Policy Brief,* February 2018. As of September 9, 2020:
http://best-nc.org/wp-content/uploads/2018/02/Transforming-Principal-Preparation-FINAL.pdf

Branch, Gregory F., Erica A. Hanushek, and Steven G. Rivkin, "Estimating the Effect of Leaders on Public Sector Productivity: The Case of School Principals," National Bureau of Economic Research, NBER Working Paper No. 17803, February 2012. As of September 6, 2020:
http://www.nber.org/papers/w17803

CAEP—*See* Council for the Accreditation of Educator Preparation.

California Commission on Teacher Credentialing, "Chapter Four: The Accreditation Cycle," *Accreditation Handbook*, Sacramento, Calif., 2016. As of September 6, 2020: https://www.ctc.ca.gov/docs/default-source/educator-prep/accred-handbook/2016/ah-chapter-04-pdf.pdf?sfvrsn=acacdda4_0

California Commission on Teacher Credentialing, "Navigating the Clear Administrative Services Credential," March 21, 2017a. As of September 6, 2020: https://www.ctc.ca.gov/educator-prep/clear-asc/default

California Commission on Teacher Credentialing, "Update on the Development of the California Administrator Performance Assessment (CalAPA) and Pilot Study and Request for a Non-Consequential Administration Year (2018–19)," 2017b.

California Commission on Teacher Credentialing, "About CalAPA: California Educator Credentialing Assessments," 2018. As of September 6, 2020: https://www.ctcexams.nesinc.com/PageView.aspx?f=GEN_AboutCalAPA.html

California Commission on Teacher Credentialing, *California Administrator Performance Assessment (CalAPA) Overview: Overview of Leadership Cycles and Rubrics Version 03,* Sacramento, Calif., 2019a. As of September 6, 2020: http://www.ctcexams.nesinc.com/Content/Docs/CalAPA_Assessment_Overview.pdf

California Commission on Teacher Credentialing, *Commission Meeting Agenda, August 1–2, 2019, 2A: Proposed Adoption of the Passing Score Standard for the California Administrator Performance Assessment*, August 2019b. As of September 30, 2020: https://www.ctc.ca.gov/commission/agendas/2019-08/august-2019-commission-meeting

California Commission on Teacher Credentialing, "Administrator Preparation in California," 2020a. As of September 6, 2020: https://www.ctc.ca.gov/educator-prep/asc

California Commission on Teacher Credentialing, *Common Standards Review*, Sacramento, Calif., 2020b. As of September 6, 2020: https://www.ctc.ca.gov/educator-prep/common-standards-review

California Department of Education, *Greatness by Design*, Sacramento, Calif., 2012. As of September 6, 2020: http://www.cde.ca.gov/eo/in/documents/greatnessfinal.pdf

California Department of Education, "21st Century California School Leadership Academy," 2020. As of September 6, 2020: https://www.cde.ca.gov/pd/ai/ca21csla.asp

Capano, Gilberto, and Michael Howlett, "The Knowns and Unknowns of Policy Instrument Analysis: Policy Tools and the Current Research Agenda on Policy Mixes," *SAGE Open*, January 24, 2020. As of September 6, 2020: https://doi.org/10.1177/2158244019900568

Chiang, Eva, Catherine Jaynes, Anne Wicks Humphrey, Abby Hoak-Morton, Eric Larsen, Matthew Clifford, Mariann Lemke, Dana Chambers, and Andrew Swanlund, *Developing Leaders: The Importance—and the Challenges—of Evaluating Principal Preparation Program,* Dallas, Tex.: George W. Bush Institute and American Institutes for Research, 2016. As of September 6, 2020: http://gwbcenter.imgix.net/Resources/GWBI_AIR-EvaluatingPrincipalPrep.pdf

Clifford, Matthew, and Steven Ross, *Designing Principal Evaluation Systems: Research to Guide Decision-Making, An Executive Summary of Current Research*, Washington, D.C.: American Institutes for Research, 2011. As of October 12, 2020:
http://www.naesp.org/sites/default/files/PrincipalEvaluation_ExecutiveSummary.pdf

Connecticut Education Association, "Connecticut Education Association: Idea of Standards Board Gets Public Airing," November 15, 2011.

Connecticut State Department of Education, *Resource Guide for New Administrators*, September 2018. As of September 6, 2020:
https://portal.ct.gov/-/media/SDE/Talent_Office/New_Administrators_CSDE_Resource_Guide-September_2018.pdf?la=en

Council for the Accreditation of Educator Preparation, "Accreditation Cycle," 2019a. As of September 6, 2020:
http://caepnet.org/accreditation/caep-accreditation/accreditation-cycle

Council for the Accreditation of Educator Preparation, "Program Review Overview," 2019b. As of September 6, 2020:
http://caepnet.org/accreditation/caep-accreditation/program-review-options

Council for the Accreditation of Educator Preparation, "State Partnership Agreements," 2019c. As of September 6, 2020:
http://caepnet.org/working-together/state-partners

Council of Chief State School Officers, *Transparency in Stakeholder Engagement: A Tool to Help Demonstrate How Stakeholders Informed the State ESSA Plan,* Washington, D.C., 2020. As of September 6, 2020:
https://ccsso.org/resource-library/transparency-stakeholder-engagement

CTC—*See* California Commission on Teacher Credentialing.

Darling-Hammond, Linda, Maria E. Hyler, and Madelyn Gardner, *Effective Teacher Professional Development*, Palo Alto, Calif.: Learning Policy Institute, June 2017. As of September 6, 2020:
https://learningpolicyinstitute.org/sites/default/files/product-files/Effective_Teacher_Professional_Development_REPORT.pdf

Davis, Jacquelyn, *Improving University Principal Preparation Programs: Five Themes from the Field,* New York: The Wallace Foundation, 2016. As of September 6, 2020:
https://www.wallacefoundation.org/knowledge-center/pages/improving-university-principal-preparation-programs.aspx

Dedoose, web application for managing, analyzing, and presenting qualitative and mixed method research data, Los Angeles, Calif.: SocioCultural Research Consultants, LLC, 2018. As of September 15, 2020:
https://www.dedoose.com

Denzin, Norman K., *Sociological Methods: A Sourcebook,* Chicago: Aldine Transaction, 2006.

Denzin, Norman K., and Yvonna S. Lincoln, *Collecting and Interpreting Qualitative Materials*, Thousand Oaks, Calif.: SAGE Publications, 2003.

Education Development Center, *Quality Measures, Tenth Edition*, 2018. As of September 17, 2018:
http://www.wallacefoundation.org/knowledge-center/Documents/Principal-Preparation-Program-Quality-Self-Assessment-Rubrics.pdf

Educational Testing Service, *The SLS Study Companion: School Leaders Licensure Assessment*, 2018a. As of September 6, 2020:
https://www.ets.org/s/sls/pdf/6990.pdf

Educational Testing Service, *The* Praxis *Study Companion: Educational Leadership Administration and Supervision*, 2018b. As of September 6, 2020:
https://www.ets.org/s/praxis/pdf/5412.pdf

Florida Department of Education, "Professional Learning Programs," webpage, undated. As of September 30, 2020:
http://www.fldoe.org/teaching/professional-dev/professional-learning-programs.stml

Florida Department of Education, "Approval of Level I Educational Leadership Programs Transcript," January 31, 2017. As of October 12, 2020:
http://www.fldoe.org/core/fileparse.php/7502/urlt/ALIELPWTranscript.pdf

Florida Department of Education, "6A-5.081 Approval of School Leadership Programs," 2018. As of September 6, 2020:
https://www.flrules.org/gateway/ruleno.asp?id=6A-5.081

Florida Department of Education, "Professional Development in Florida," 2020. As of September 6, 2020:
http://www.fldoe.org/teaching/professional-dev/professional-dev-resources-technical-a.stml

Florida Legislature, 1012.98 School Community Professional Development Act, 2019.

Fry, Betty, Gene Bottoms, and Kathy O'Neill, *The Principal Internship: How Can We Get It Right?* Atlanta, Ga.: Southern Regional Education Board, 2005. As of September 6, 2020:
https://www.sreb.org/publication/principal-internship

Fuller, Edward J., Liz Hollingworth, and Jing Lui, "Evaluating State Principal Evaluation Plans Across the United States," *Journal of Research on Leadership Education*, Vol. 10, No. 3, 2015, pp. 164–192.

Gates, Susan M., Matthew D. Baird, Benjamin K. Master, and Emilio R. Chavez-Herrerias, *Principal Pipelines: What Public School Districts Report Doing and What They Want to Do to Improve School Leadership,* Santa Monica, Calif.: RAND Corporation, RR-2666-WF, 2019. As of September 6, 2020:
http://www.rand.org/pubs/research_reports/RR2666.html

Gates, Susan M., Julia H. Kaufman, Sy Doan, Andrea Prado Tuma, and Deborah Kim, *Taking Stock of Principal Pipelines: A Feasible, Affordable, and Effective Way for Districts to Improve Schools,* Santa Monica, Calif.: RAND Corporation, RR-A274-1, 2020. As of September 6, 2020:
http://www.rand.org/pubs/research_reports/RRA274-1.html

Georgia Assessments for the Certification of Educators, "About the Performance Assessment for School Leaders (PASL)," 2020. As of September 6, 2020:
https://gace.ets.org/pasl/about?WT.ac=GACE_pasl_33082_151209

Georgia Department of Education, "160-5-1-.37 Teacher and Leader Evaluations," 2016. As of September 6, 2020:
https://www.gadoe.org/External-Affairs-and-Policy/State-Board-of-Education/SBOE%20Rules/160-5-1-.37.pdf

Georgia Governor's Office of Student Achievement, "Governor's School Leadership Academy: Aspiring Principal Program," 2020a. As of September 6, 2020:
https://gosa.georgia.gov/programs-initiatives/governors-school-leadership-academy/governors-school-leadership-academy-0

Georgia Governor's Office of Student Achievement, "Governor's School Leadership Academy (GSLA)," 2020b. As of September 6, 2020:
https://gosa.georgia.gov/programs-initiatives/governors-school-leadership-academy

Georgia Professional Standards Commission, "Georgia Ethics for Educational Leadership Assessment," 2019. As of September 6, 2020:
https://gace.ets.org/ethics/about/educational_leadership

Georgia Professional Standards Commission, "505-2-.36 Renewal Requirements," January 1, 2020. As of September 6, 2020:
https://www.gapsc.com/Rules/Current/Certification/505-2-.36.pdf

Granados, Alex, "What's Happened with Principals in the Last 5 Years," EdNC, January 6, 2020 As of September 6, 2020:
https://www.ednc.org/whats-happened-with-principals-in-the-last-5-years/

Grissom, Jason A., and Brendan Bartanen, *Assessing Equity in School Leadership in California.* Stanford University, Policy Analysis for California Education (PACE), 2018. As of September 6, 2020:
https://gettingdowntofacts.com/sites/default/files/2018-09/GDTFII_Report_Grissom.pdf

Grissom, Jason A., Demetra Kalogrides, and Susanna Loeb, "Using Student Test Scores to Measure Principal Performance," *Educational Evaluation and Policy Analysis,* Vol. 37, No. 1, 2015, pp. 3–28.

Grissom, Jason A., Hajime Mitani, and Richard S. L. Blissett, "Principal Licensure Exams and Future Job Performance: Evidence from the School Leaders Licensure Assessment," *Educational Evaluation and Policy Analysis,* Vol. 39, No. 2, 2017, pp. 248–280.

Grissom, Jason A., Hajime Mitani, and David S. Woo, "Principal Preparation Programs and Principal Outcomes," *Educational Administration Quarterly,* Vol. 55, No. 1, 2019, pp. 73–115.

Haller, Alicia, Erika Hunt, and Debra Baron, "Applying the Advocacy Coalition Framework to the Policy Change Process in Illinois," in Erika Hunt, Lisa Hood, Alicia Haller, and Maureen Kincaid, eds., *Reforming Principal Preparation at the State Level: Perspectives on Policy Reform from Illinois,* Abingdon, UK: Routledge, 2019a, pp. 28–61.

Haller, Alicia, Erika Hunt, and Debra Baron, "Setting the Stage for State Policy Change Involving Principal Preparation in Illinois: The What and How," in Erika Hunt, Lisa Hood, Alicia Haller, and Maureen Kincaid, eds., *Reforming Principal Preparation at the State Level: Perspectives on Policy Reform from Illinois,* Abingdon, UK: Routledge, 2019b.

Herman, Rebecca, Susan M. Gates, Aziza Arifkhanova, Mark Barrett, Andriy Bega, Emilio R. Chavez-Herrerias, Eugeniu Han, Mark Harris, Katya Migacheva, Rachel Ross, Jennifer T. Leschitz, and Stephani L. Wrabel, *School Leadership Interventions Under the Every Student Succeeds Act: Evidence Review—Updated and Expanded,* Santa Monica, Calif.: RAND Corporation, RR-1550-3-WF, 2017. As of September 6, 2020:
https://www.rand.org/pubs/research_reports/RR1550-3.html

Hess, Frederick M., and Andrew P. Kelly, *Learning to Lead? What Gets Taught in Principal Preparation Programs,* Olin Foundation, 2007. As of September 6, 2020:
https://files.eric.ed.gov/fulltext/ED485999.pdf

Hitt, Dallas Hambrick, Pamela D. Tucker, and Michelle D. Young, *The Professional Pipeline for Educational Leadership: A White Paper Developed to Inform the Work of the National Policy Board for Educational Administration,* Charlottesville, Va.: National Policy Board for Educational Administration, 2012.

Howlett, Michael, "The Criteria for Effective Policy Design: Character and Context in Policy Instrument Choice," *Journal of Asian Public Policy,* Vol. 11, No. 3, 2017, pp. 245–266.

Howley, Caitlyn, and Keith M. Sturges, "Building Capacity in State Education Agencies: Using Organizational Theory to Guide Technical Assistance," *Journal of Organizational Theory in Education,* Vol. 3, No. 1, 2018, p. 1–19.

Hunt, Erika, Lisa Hood, Alicia Haller, and Maureen Kincaid, eds., *Reforming Principal Preparation at the State Level: Perspectives on Policy Reform from Illinois*, Abingdon, UK: Routledge, 2019.

Johnston, William R., Julia H. Kaufman, and Lindsey E. Thompson, *Support for Instructional Leadership: Supervision, Mentoring, and Professional Development for U.S. School Leaders: Findings from the American School Leader Panel,* Santa Monica, Calif.: RAND Corporation, RR-1580-1-WF, 2016. As of September 20, 2020:
https://www.rand.org/pubs/research_reports/RR1580-1.html

Kaufman, Julia H., and Tiffany Berglund, *School Supports for Teachers' Implementation of State Standards: Findings from the American School Leader Panel,* Santa Monica, Calif.: RAND Corporation, RR-2318-BMGF, 2018. As of September 6, 2020:
https://www.rand.org/pubs/research_reports/RR2318.html

Kentucky Department of Education, "Principal Partnership Project (P3)," 2019. As of September 6, 2020:
https://education.ky.gov/teachers/Pages/Principal-Partnership-Project-(P3).aspx

Kentucky Legislature, 704 KAR 3:035. Annual Professional Development Plan, 2020.

Kingdon, John W., *Agendas, Alternatives, and Public Policies,* Boston, Mass.: Little, Brown, 1984.

Lead Connecticut, "Turnaround Principal Program," 2020. As of September 6, 2020:
http://www.leadconnecticut.org/services-programs/turnaround-principal-program/

Learning Forward, *Standards for Professional Learning,* Oxford, Ohio, 2011.

Leithwood, Kenneth, Karen Seashore Louis, Stephen Anderson, and Kyla Wahlstrom, *Review of Research: How Leadership Influences Student Learning,* New York: The Wallace Foundation, 2004. As of September 6, 2020:
https://www.wallacefoundation.org/knowledge-center/Documents/How-Leadership-Influences-Student-Learning.pdf

Liebowitz, David D., and Lorna Porter, "The Effect of Principal Behaviors on Student, Teacher, and School Outcomes: A Systematic Review and Meta-Analysis of the Empirical Literature," *Review of Educational Research,* Vol. 89, No. 5, 2019, pp. 785–827.

Lincoln, Yvonna S., and Egon G. Guba, *Naturalistic Inquiry,* Newbury Park, Calif.: SAGE Publications, 1985.

Manna, Paul, *Developing Excellent School Principals to Advance Teaching and Learning: Considerations for State Policy,* New York: The Wallace Foundation, 2015. As of September 6, 2020:
https://www.wallacefoundation.org/knowledge-center/pages/developing-excellent-school-principals.aspx

McDonnell, Lorraine M., and Richard F. Elmore, "Getting the Job Done: Alternative Policy Instruments," *Educational Evaluation and Policy Analysis,* Vol. 9, No. 2, 1987, pp. 133–152.

Miles, Matthew B., and A. Michael Huberman, *Qualitative Data Analysis: An Expanded Sourcebook,* Thousand Oaks, Calif.: SAGE Publications, 1994.

Moffitt, Susan L., Matthew J. Lyddon, Domingo Morel, Michaela Krug O'Neill, Kelly B. Smith, Cadence Willse, and David K. Cohen, *State Structures for Instructional Support in California,* Stanford University, Policy Analysis for California Education, 2018. As of September 6, 2020:
https://gettingdowntofacts.com/sites/default/files/2018-09/GDTFII_Report_Moffitt_structures_0.pdf

National Association of State Boards of Education, "State Education Governance Matrix," March 2020. As of September 6, 2020:
https://nasbe.nyc3.digitaloceanspaces.com/2020/03/Governance-matrix-March-2020.pdf

National Association of State Directors of Teacher Education and Certification, "Professional Educator Standards Board Association," 2019. As of October 12, 2020:
https://www.nasdtec.net/general/custom.asp?page=PESBA&DGPCrPg=1&DGPCrSrt=7D

National Center for Teacher Quality, "Teacher and Principal Evaluation Policy," 2019. As of September 6, 2020:
https://www.nctq.org/pages/State-of-the-States-2019:-Teacher-and-Principal-Evaluation-Policy

National Conference of State Legislatures, *School Leadership: A Key to Student Success*, 2020. As of October 12, 2020:
https://www.ncsl.org/Portals/1/Documents/educ/School-Leadership_v02.pdf

National Policy Board for Educational Administration, *Professional Standards for Educational Leaders,* Reston, Va., 2015. As of September 6, 2020:
http://www.npbea.org/wp-content/uploads/2017/06/Professional-Standards-for-Educational-Leaders_2015.pdf

New Leaders, *Prioritizing Leadership: An Analysis of State ESSA Plans,* New York, 2018. As of September 6, 2020:
https://files.eric.ed.gov/fulltext/ED591503.pdf

North Carolina Department of Public Instruction, "Compensation for Public School Employees," 2019. As of September 6, 2020:
https://www.dpi.nc.gov/districts-schools/district-operations/financial-and-business-services/compensation-public-school-employees

North Carolina State Board of Education, "Policy TCED-015: School Administrator Preparation Programs," 2018.

North Carolina State Education Assistance Authority, *Rules and Regulations: North Carolina Principal Fellows Program*, Research Triangle Park, N.C., 1999. As of September 6, 2020:
http://www.ncseaa.edu/pdf/PFP.pdf

Principal Academy, "School of Education: School Leadership Institute," 2020. As of May 2020:
https://education.wm.edu/centers/sli/events/Principal%20Academy/index.php

Professional Educator Standards Boards Association, *2017 Educator Standards Board Report,* Washington, D.C., 2017. As of September 6, 2020:
https://cdn.ymaws.com/www.nasdtec.net/resource/collection/97608343-51F6-44F1-B39D-093A3B2F930F/ISB_Report_2017_Update_(Final_Edition).pdf

Public Law 89-10, Elementary and Secondary Education Act, April 11, 1965.

Public Law 107-110, No Child Left Behind Act, January 8, 2002.

Public Law 114-95, Every Student Succeeds Act, December 10, 2015.

Punch, Keith F., *Introduction to Social Research: Quantitative and Qualitative Approaches,* London: SAGE Publications, 2014.

Rowland, C., *Principal Professional Development: New Opportunities for a Renewed State Focus,* Washington, D.C.: American Institutes for Research, 2017. As of October 12, 2020:
https://www.air.org/sites/default/files/downloads/report/Principal-Professional-Development-New-Opportunities-State-Focus-February-2017.pdf

Ryan, Gery W., and H. Russell Bernard, "Techniques to Identify Themes," *Field Methods,* Vol. 15, No. 1, 2003, pp. 85–109.

School Educational Leadership Enhancement Committee Task Force, *SELECT Report*, 2018, Not available to the general public.

Scott, Deven, "50-State Comparison: School Leader Certification and Preparation Program," Education Commission of the States, 2018. As of September 6, 2020:
https://www.ecs.org/50-state-comparison-school-leader-certification-and-preparation-programs/

SELECT—*See* School Educational Leadership Enhancement Committee Task Force.

Shelton, S., *School Leadership: A Key to Student Success*, Denver, Colo.: National Conference of State Legislatures , 2013.

Sherman, Whitney H., and B. Cunningham, "Improving Administrator Preparation and Practice Through Well-Designed Internships," paper presented at the annual convention for the University Council of Educational Administration, San Antonio, Tex., November 2006.

Shroff, Monal R., Sonya J. Jones, Edward A. Frongillo, and Michael Howlett, "Policy Instruments Used by States Seeking to Improve School Food Environments," *American Journal of Public Health*, Vol. 102, No. 2, 2012, pp. 222–229.

Smarick, Andy, and Juliet Squire, *The State Education Agency: At the Helm, Not the Oar,* Washington D.C.: Thomas B. Fordham Institute, 2014. As of September 6, 2020:
https://files.eric.ed.gov/fulltext/ED553706.pdf

Smylie, Mark A., and Joseph Murphy, "School Leader Standards from ISLLC to PSEL: Notes on Their Development and the Work Ahead," *UCEA Review*, Fall 2018, pp. 24–28. As of September 6, 2020:
http://www.npbea.org/wp-content/uploads/2018/10/Smylie-Murphy-2018-School-leader-standards-from-ISLLC-to-PSEL-UCEA-Review-article-only.pdf

Strauss, Anselm, and Juliet Corbin, *Basics of Qualitative Research: Grounded Theory Procedures and Techniques,* London: SAGE Publications, 1990.

Strauss, Anselm, and Juliet Corbin, "Grounded Theory Methodology: An Overview," in Norman K. Denzin and Yvonna S. Lincoln, eds., *Handbook of Qualitative Research*, London: SAGE Publications, 1994, pp. 273–285.

TNTP, *The Mirage: Confronting the Hard Truth About Our Quest for Teacher Development*, Brooklyn, N.Y., 2015.

Turnbull, Brenda J., Derek L. Riley, and Jaclyn R. MacFarlane, *Building a Stronger Principalship*, Vol. 2, *Cultivating Talent Through a Principal Pipeline,* Washington, D.C.: Policy Studies Associates, Inc., December 2013. As of September 6, 2020:
https://www.wallacefoundation.org/knowledge-center/pages/building-a-stronger-principalship-vol-2-cultivating-talent-through-a-principal-pipeline.aspx

UCEA—*See* University Council for Educational Administration.

University Council for Educational Administration, "National Educational Leadership Preparation (NELP) Standards," 2018. As of September 6, 2020:
http://www.ucea.org/initiatives/1523/

University of North Carolina System, "UNC Educator Quality Dashboard," 2020. Retrieved May 2020,
http://eqdashboard.northcarolina.edu/

U.S. Department of Education, National Center for Education Statistics, "Elementary/Secondary Information System," web application, undated. As of September 30, 2020:
https://nces.ed.gov/ccd/elsi/

U.S. Department of Education, National Center for Education Statistics, Common Core of Data (CCD), "Local Education Agency (School District) Universe Survey," 2016–2017 v.1a, 2017a.

U.S. Department of Education, National Center for Education Statistics, Common Core of Data (CCD), "Local Education Agency (School District) Universe Survey Geographic Data (EDGE)," 2016–2017 v.1a, 2017b.

Virginia Department of Education, *Virginia Licensure Renewal Manual,* Richmond, Va., 2019. As of September 6, 2020:
http://www.doe.virginia.gov/teaching/licensure/licensure-renewal-manual.docx

Virginia Department of Education, "Professional Learning Network," 2020. As of September 6, 2020:
http://www.doe.virginia.gov/teaching/professional-learning/professional-learning-network/index.shtml

Wang, Elaine Lin, Susan M. Gates, Rebecca Herman, Monica Mean, Rachel Perera, Tiffany Berglund, Katie Whipkey, and Megan Andrew, *Launching a Redesign of University Principal Preparation Programs: Partners Collaborate for Change,* Santa Monica, Calif.: RAND Corporation, RR-2612-WF, 2018. As of September 6, 2020:
https://www.rand.org/pubs/research_reports/RR2612

Weiss, Joann, and Patrick McGuinn, "States as Change Agents Under ESSA," *Phi Delta Kappan,* Vol. 97, No. 8, 2016, pp. 28–33.